Lineman Wayne Henry performs maintenance to power lines in 2008.

Dominion's First Century

A Legacy of Service

An operator checked oil levels on a cooling water pump at Richmond's 12th Street Power Station in the 1930s. First placed into service in 1900, the station "gave the appearance of a modern castle," according to an historian. It supplied most of the area's electricity until World War II, when it was superseded by the much-larger Chesterfield Power Station on the James River in Chester. 12th Street's hydro units were retired in 1968. Its steam units sustained flood damage during Hurricane Agnes in 1972 and were retired three years later.

Dominion's First Century

A Legacy of Service

BY HEIDI TYLINE KING

Dominion's First Century: A Legacy of Service
© 2010 Dominion Resources, Inc. All rights reserved.

Library of Congress Control Number: 2009936354
ISBN: 978-0-9768331-6-1

Produced and published by CorporateHistory.net LLC,
Hasbrouck Heights, N.J.
www.corporatehistory.net

Written by Heidi Tyline King

Edited by Marian Calabro

Cover and interior design by Timothy H. Priddy,
Communication Design, Inc., Richmond, Va.

Printed by Worth Higgins & Associates, Inc., Richmond, Va.

Printed on FSC certified paper
Cover: Productolith PTS, 12 point C1S
Text: Sterling Dull, 100#

Photography credits: All images and artifacts appear courtesy of Dominion, except those credited otherwise on page
122. Dominion expresses sincere appreciation to employees
and retirees for use of their photos and memorabilia.

Richmond employees raised their first safety flag in 1931. Winners of the company's accident elimination contests earned the right to fly the coveted banner.

TRACE THE RICH HISTORY OF VIRGINIA ENTERPRISE, and you will quickly cross paths with Dominion's many and varied antecedents. We may honestly claim to have been there at the beginning, in the late 18th century, as new lands were explored to the west, new trade worked its way to the coast, and industry began to reshape the character of Virginia and create previously unimagined potential. Ours is an altogether American story, of course — one of risk-taking, invention and determination, and how the historic roots of Dominion took hold. Our enduring legacy well justifies the effort reflected in these pages.

In fits and starts, Dominion's history begins in 1785, as assorted Virginia entrepreneurs labor to establish successful businesses, some with happier results than others. The modern story really emerges in 1909, as Dominion enters the brave, new world of electric power generation — and not for the sake of illumination, either. Our predecessors wanted to get Richmond moving, to build more efficient and effective transportation in a rapidly growing urban community. Thus, Richmond became the birthplace of the streetcar. After that, it was only a matter of time before the power generated to move the trolleys would be put to the service of lighting the city.

In practice, from that point on, Dominion has seldom looked back, as we have constantly pursued the next, best technology for generating and transmitting power, ever safer procedures, reliability unrivaled by any energy company in the land, and excellence throughout our growing organization.

Pausing for a look back, though, has great value for us all. The teamwork we call One Dominion developed neither by happenstance nor accident; instead, it is the accumulated result of committed employees who have built on the work of generations before. These pages chronicle the ingenuity, diligence, and dogged resolution of Dominion's people. We can read it with a justifiable sense of pride.

Tom Farrell

Thomas F. Farrell II
Chairman, President, and CEO

Soon after their development in 1948, mercury vapor streetlights began replacing incandescent lights. They were much brighter than their predecessors, an improvement that was celebrated in 1954 in Kilmarnock, Virginia, with a parade featuring the high school marching band and a speech by the mayor.

CHAPTER 1

"The Whole Town Twinkled"

> COLD FIGURES do not measure the human importance of electric power in our present social order. Electricity is no longer a luxury, it is a definite necessity.
>
> FRANKLIN D. ROOSEVELT

Octogenarian K. B. Tillman can still remember the magic of electricity.

When he was a boy in the 1930s, his family would hop into their Model T every Saturday evening to make the seven-mile jaunt down Route 6 to Columbia, Virginia, from their home in Bremo Bluff. Standing on the floorboard in the backseat and looking over his father's shoulder as he drove along, K. B. waited for the moment they would top the hill on the outskirts of town, when the gray shadows of early evening would give way to a blanket of light illuminating the valley below.

"The whole town twinkled," he remembered. "We'd beg to ride by the beer joint, where the entire front was lit up, and by the church on the hill that had the prettiest little lights in the windows. When we'd head for home later that night, you couldn't believe how dark it really was back in the country."

At the turn of the 20th century, most towns and cities had electricity. Richmond's electric streetlights date to 1881, seven years after the invention of the light bulb, when they were temporarily strung as a novelty to celebrate the Battle of Yorktown Centennial. Two years later, despite protests that electricity was a "dangerous and frightful thing which would kill innocent people,"

the city erected poles and wire to light the streets permanently. England's Prince of Wales, who later became King Edward VII, was a guest of the city for the occasion.

The story was different on Virginia's farms. In 1934, only seven out of 100 farms had electricity.

Virginia's state capitol, located in Richmond, was designed by Thomas Jefferson. Constructed in 1785, the building was outfitted with running water in 1832, gas lights in 1851, and telephones and electricity in the late 1800s. At that time, gas was considered more reliable than electricity, so light fixtures throughout were equipped to use both.

DOMINION'S CORPORATE ANCESTRY

What's an electric company doing selling ice and home mortgages, not to mention operating or developing hotels, amusement parks, "public watering places," and neighborhoods? Throughout its history, there has been a diverse mix of companies created, acquired, or merged into Dominion's corporate family tree. Some were successful; others failed or were discontinued, but all offered valuable lessons that strengthened the company and refocused attention on its core business.

Canal development/water rights

Ice company

Street railway (trolley car) construction company

Cotton oil press mill

Electric distribution and transmission

Natural gas production

Natural gas distribution, transmission, and storage

Utility power production

Merchant power production

Railroad operations

Trolley car operations

Real estate development

Iron smelting and general foundry business

Bar iron, horse shoes, and nail company

Hotel and amusement park development

Steam ferry operations

Viaduct and bridge construction and operations

Laundry company

Grain milling company

Nuclear power

Coal mining

Investment management services

Mortgage and home equity loan company

Telecom business

Gas and oil exploration and production

It wasn't cheap, and it wasn't easy to install, especially on farms like that of the Tillmans, located far from the power lines strung along the main roads. To alleviate the problems farmers faced in obtaining affordable electricity, the government created the Rural Electrification Administration (REA) in 1935. President Franklin D. Roosevelt felt electricity had the power to vastly improve the lives of rural Americans; the REA approached electrification as an important social need.

Consequently, electricity spread slowly across the rural areas of the Commonwealth, down one dirt road at a time. "We had oil lamps, and we had to wash the globes because they would get smutty after three or four days — and on top of that were fumes," remembered 76-year-old Moses Foster Sr., whose Prince Edward County farm was powered in the early 1940s. "We suffered quite a bit from that, and we were glad to see electricity come. We were quite excited to know that we didn't have to charge batteries anymore or churn up and down to make butter."

Not until 1950 did 90 percent of farms have electricity. But country or city, when electrification finally arrived, it revolutionized a way of life — *that* was its magic.

This is the story of the Virginia company that has made the magic happen for the past 100 years. By now, there are few people like K. B. Tillman and Moses Foster who remember life before electricity — before Virginia Electric and Power Company, better known as VEPCO. Nor would any Virginians foresee the transformative economic, social, and political journey that their state and VEPCO were poised to begin together. Today the company is Dominion, a household word across the Commonwealth, the mid-Atlantic, Midwest, and Northeast; a fixture on Wall Street; a recognized corporate philanthropist; an industry leader and trusted provider of customer service, shareholder value, and environmental stewardship.

Dominion's storied history is intertwined with that of the Commonwealth's, and who better to tell this incredible story than employees, retirees,

Richmond's canals started in the 1780s as part of George Washington's vision for a national transportation system. The canals allowed cargo transport by the flat-bottomed bateaux to bypass Richmond's rapids and reach ocean-faring ships below. Heavily damaged in the Civil War, the canals were replaced by railroads, which were laid on canal towpaths. Today portions of the canals have been restored as part of Richmond's Canal Walk.

customers, shareholders, and friends? Their individual tales collectively record the company's history with a depth and intimacy that a traditional history book cannot. They also illustrate how Dominion orchestrated its remarkable 100-year run: by making hard decisions at critical times, embracing change when needed to circumvent obstacles, exuding a "Work Hard, Play Hard" attitude, and, above all, staying true to the core values of safety, excellence, ethics, and teamwork of One Dominion.

THE UPPER APPOMATTOX COMPANY

Dominion's corporate family tree has deep roots tangled by acquisitions, mergers, and newly created companies, as well as those sold or dissolved. The oldest forerunner of company ancestry stretches back to the early days of the American republic, when several forward-thinking businessmen founded the Upper Appomattox Company in 1795. Originally chartered on December 17, 1787, as the Appomattox Trustees, the canal company dabbled in several businesses, including flour and cotton mills. It also promoted navigation and canal operation on the Appomattox River for the sake of hauling rum and tobacco from the highlands to Tidewater and Hampton Roads.

Even in its infancy, the company looked after employees, sometimes going so far as to intervene in personal matters. Consider these cryptic entries made in early company journals about an unfortunate worker named Hampton:

> *One box of pills for Hampton.*
> *…to doctor for bleeding Hampton.*
> *Blankets for Hampton.*
> *Medicine for Hampton.*
> *Coffin and funeral expenses for Hampton.*

There are payment records for the extraction of teeth, one grindstone, a claw hammer, blanket and bottle of wine, and doctor's fees of "3 pounds, 12 pence for curing Alex of venereal bubo." The Upper Appomattox Company also took care of its trustees, providing a small barrel of whisky for each directors' meeting.

In 1888, the company bought several hydroelectric stations and a steam power facility on the Appomattox River, the earliest indication of electricity interests by one of Dominion's forebears. The trustees saw the new market for electricity as an opportunity to get out of debt using a lucrative, low-overhead system based on water-driven electrical generators. Despite its diverse holdings and aspirations, the company failed to make much money. In 1899, portions of the Upper Appomattox Company were sold. The electrical division and its water rights were absorbed by the newly formed Southside Railway Development Company.

JUNE 29, 1909: "A RED-LETTER DATE"

Curiously, trolley cars fueled the electric business. In 1888, the same year the Upper Appomattox Company ventured into the electricity market, the Richmond Union Passenger Railway Company became the first in the nation to successfully operate an electrical trolley system. Over time, this company, along with the Southside Railway Development Company, was rolled into one entity, the Virginia Passenger and Power Company. That company was owned primarily by Frank Jay Gould and Helen Gould. The son and daughter of the powerful Wall Street financier Jay Gould of 1869 "Black Friday" notoriety, they were established businesspeople in their own right. Like its predecessors, however, the company soon met with financial peril, spurred by the national financial panic of 1907.

ABOVE LEFT: Frank Jay Gould and his sister, Helen, shared investments, but Frank was the financier, Helen the philanthropist. *ABOVE*: "Modern" trucks such as this Virginia Railway and Power Company Electric Service truck from the early 1900s were eventually used for heavy transports, but even in the 1940s, nothing had yet to take the place of oxen teams for transporting 60-foot poles through swamplands where tractors would bog down and stall.

RICHMOND ON RAILS

Electric trolleys came to Richmond in the second half of the 1800s. The earliest cars had been carriages pulled by teams of horses or mules throughout the city as public transportation.

The switch from manual to electric power came on November 7, 1887, when Frank Sprague successfully electrified the Richmond Union Passenger Railway Company. Sprague, a former assistant of Thomas Edison, had implemented the use of efficient mathematical calculations in Edison's lab, saving the inventor thousands of hours of needless tinkering. He also improved Edison's central station distribution model for electricity. Like Edison, Sprague was also an inventor with a keen interest in electricity, and his experiments on powering main supply systems and electrical traction led to the idea of supplying electricity to trolley cars through overhead wires.

Sprague used the technology to power Richmond's street cars. Spectators gathered that first day to watch the monumental event, but with the city's sharp curves and steep grades, the car faltered, bucked, and finally stalled before topping a hill. In a loud voice, Sprague called for the "instruments" to repair it. Only after the crowd had melted away did his assistants produce these tools — four mules to tow the car to the barn. Despite setbacks, Sprague's system was perfected and Richmond became the first city in the country to have a successfully operated commercial electric street railway, opening in January 1888 with 10 cars in operation.

Trolley car drivers were well-respected in the community and, to some degree, could be considered predecessors of the company's public relations department. Early company newsletters are filled with letters from customers praising their "cheerfulness and genuine politeness to all alike." Said one: "Several times I have noticed him help some old, feeble person from his car, with true gentlemanly

politeness, and I have also noticed other extra attentions given his passengers by him." Another commendation for a remarkable stop at an intersection stated that had a conductor's "cool judgment failed him, it would probably have caused the death of a two-year-old child."

The drivers were also heroes. Collisions with automobiles stalled on the tracks were common, and newspaper accounts heralded drivers for averting potential disaster with quick maneuvering when a car or person crossed illegally in front of the trolley.

ABOVE LEFT: Virginia Electric and Power Company trolley tokens from the Portsmouth, Norfolk, and Richmond divisions. *ABOVE*: Trolley cars rolled through Richmond for almost 100 years. This photograph, looking west from 11th Street, shows a car along Main Street in 1900.
RIGHT: Motorman W. E. Blanton avoided a serious collision by "keeping a level head and using it."

Public Service News

SAFETY FIRST

EFFICIENT SERVICE

Vol. VIII.—No. 3   September 17, 1922   Whole No. 172

Published by Virginia Railway and Power Company

MOTORMAN BLANTON EXHIBITS SKILL IN AVOIDING SERIOUS ACCIDENT

Eye-Witnesses Become Nervous As They Look On—They Imagine All Kind of Things—But Blanton Saves the Day.

Motorman W. E. Blanton, operating from the Seventh and Perry Terminal, wins a place in the "Hall of Fame".

On the morning of August 26, Mr. Blanton demonstrated that "a careful man is the best safety device known" and that serious accidents can often be avoided by keeping a level head and using it.

Mr. Blanton was operating his car up Seventh Street, north of Main, and when he reached Seventh and Franklin Streets, he noticed that the car ahead of him had, for some reason, become uncontrollable and was sliding backward down the steep grade of Seventh Street, between Grace and Franklin, at a dizzy rate of speed.

A collision was inevitable.

If he had been inclined to observe always the first law of nature, that of self-preservation, he would have jumped from his platform, but that wasn't the make-up of Motorman Blanton. His twenty years of experience in public service had long since impressed him with the responsibility for the lives of others which were in his keeping. Hence, in this perilous moment, too, his first thought was for his passengers. He gauged the speed with which the on-coming car was approaching his car and at the proper time reversed his car and when the impact came the damage was only a slightly impaired fender on the maneuvering car. There were, of course, several cases of "shattered nerves" on

W. E. BLANTON.

the part of by-standers on the sidewalk who witnessed the incident, one of them stating afterwards he became so excited that he broke the lace in his shoe.

All witnesses warmly commended the presence of mind and ingenuity of Motorman Blanton.

(Continued on Page 3.)

By Being at the Door to Alight When Car Stops Speeds Up Service!

The hours required for the job, however, were backbreaking. W. R. Armstrong, a former driver who began when the company still operated horse cars, described a typical day in an October 1927 *Vepcovian* article: "We went on duty at 6 o'clock a.m. and working until 9 o'clock p.m. with no relief. Fifteen hours was called a day's work. We had to eat our meals in the 10 minutes at the end of the line."

As streetcars gained popularity, the company began acquiring other street rail companies. As late as 1910, the company's electric earnings were only $614,000, while its income from transportation was $1,444,000. The only real competition was from jitneys, independently owned vehicles that ran haphazardly without schedule or regulation. Only in the 1920s would the pendulum swing from transportation to electric light and power.

The beginning of the end of the trolley cars came in 1922. State Supreme Court Justice Willis D. Miller observed from the window of his office that so many automobiles downtown carried so few people. A bus system similar to one he had seen in New York would be more efficient than autos or trolleys, he believed, so he rallied a few partners and opened the Richmond Rapid Transit Company. A 1931 editorial in the *Norfolk Ledger-Dispatch* noted that:

Some buses are mighty big for narrow streets; sometimes they are driven very fast; sometimes their mechanical equipment makes it possible for them to stop too quickly for the safety of vehicles following behind. But with all this and all that, buses rather than trolley cars — two to one.

In 1944, VEPCO was ordered by the Securities and Exchange Commission to confine its activities to the electric business. The company sold the trolleys to the Virginia Transit Company, which immediately began motorizing the system. On November 25, 1949, a group of 10 streetcars coming off Hull-Highland Park paraded west on Main Street to the car barns on their last run in the city.

In 2009, some 60 years after the trolleys disappeared, Richmonders continue to harbor nostalgic memories of the VEPCO trolley cars of yesteryear. Benjamin J. Lambert III, an optometrist, Dominion

board member, and former Virginia senator, remembered riding the trolley with his brothers and friends. "When I was a boy in the 1940s, we would hop aboard the trolley that used to come out to the University of Richmond. We'd go downtown and could stay out pretty late because they ran until midnight or one in the morning."

Lovic Davis was a legacy employee whose grandfather, Luke Thaxton, worked for the company as a trolley driver. "When I went to work for VEPCO, he [my grandfather] went into his desk and pulled out an engraved brass switch key with VARWPCO, which stands for Virginia Railway and Power

Company," explained Davis. "He used it to unlock the switch boxes, and he wanted me to have it since I was going to work for the company, too." Davis retired as a lead project designer in Richmond after 38 years; the key remains one of his treasured possessions. ■

ABOVE LEFT: Luke Thaxton's brass switch key. ABOVE RIGHT: A 1939 weekly trolley pass. ABOVE: Tough as trolley drivers were, Lovic Davis remembered his grandfather, Luke Thaxton (pictured at far right), telling a story about driving the trolley during the 1918 flu epidemic. So many people were dying that some funerals would be held at night. On a particularly dark night when Thaxton was no more than 19, he drove out to Hollywood Cemetery to pick up a group of mourners. As he sat and waited in the dark, the moaning and crying from the funeral spooked him so much that he jumped into the trolley and drove it back empty to Grayland Avenue, leaving the mourners stranded.

VEPCO employees have a long history of mixing work with a little play, even if suits and hats were standard dress. This photograph was snapped at a 1925 event. *From left to right*: W. L. Goodman, L. S. Sitton, E. C. Bookman, H. Thompson, B. S. Martin, A. H. Herrman, and W. B. Jones, chauffeur.

Still intrigued by the industry's potential, the Goulds reorganized the company under orders from the United States Court for the Eastern Division of Virginia, then purchased three separate street railways in Richmond: the Richmond Traction Company, the Virginia Passenger and Power Company, and the Richmond Passenger and Power Company. On June 29, 1909, they merged the three together to create the Virginia Railway and Power Company, "probably the biggest red letter date in our history … the real beginning of the Virginia Electric and Power Company," wrote Erwin Will, chairman of the board in 1965.

The demand for electricity grew swiftly in the early 1900s, and the company kept up by acquiring other energy and railway companies in central and eastern Virginia. Soon, the Virginia Railway and Power Company was flourishing as a reputable supplier of light and power, trolley car service, and distributors of natural gas.

In the early 1920s, the company's prosperity and potential caught the attention of Stone & Webster, Inc., a New York engineering and consulting firm. In 1925, Stone & Webster purchased the Virginia Railway and Power Company and merged it with the Spotsylvania Power Company of Fredericksburg, Virginia, to create the Virginia Electric and Power Company, or VEPCO. Additionally, Stone & Webster formed Engineers Public Service Company, a subsidiary holding company, to operate VEPCO and its other energy and construction businesses. These two moves signaled a shift in core business from transportation to electricity, ushering in a new chapter in the company's history.

"WORK HARD, PLAY HARD"

A 1925 photo snapped at a company picnic shows a huge white banner draped over a utility truck. It proclaims, "Play Day and Work Day," the earliest proof that going above and beyond the call of duty — but having fun while doing so — is a century-old characteristic for Dominion employees.

Although linemen no longer climb creosote poles with bare hands, accountants have graduated from keypunch machines to computers, and meter readers scan boxes from their trucks instead of battling dogs and snakes to reach the meters on the sides of houses, these jobs remain physically and mentally grueling — the type that many folks

Bowling has been a favorite activity for employees since the early 1900s. Twelve teams competed in VEPCO's all-male Richmond league of 1928–1929. Today there are numerous bowling teams throughout the company.

would never consider as a career. The most exhausting positions usually require being on the job — and away from family — when tornadoes, hurricanes, and other natural disasters strike. Events that paralyze almost every other industry mobilize the Dominion team into action.

"In the field of work we do, it's just getting lights on," said John Croslin, a retired superintendent and safety supervisor with 35 years with the company. "I know how it is when my lights are out at home, you know? So whether we're doing it for Dominion or for Appalachian [a fellow utility], when people are out of lights … when they've got babies in the house that are cold and you get 'em back on, there's such a satisfaction in it." But when the work is done, Dominion's employees are ready to play.

Ask around and you are likely to find that some of the best memories for employees are those of

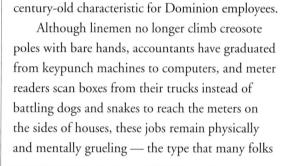

The VEPCO Glee Club of 1953 was one of the few company clubs of the era to include both men and women.

simply hanging out with friends from work. When the company was smaller, it was easier to coordinate employee socials. Playing horseshoes, swimming, building floats for hometown parades, holding Bible study classes, performing plays, and getting together for wiener roasts, company hunts, pie-eating contests, and "all-day-and-part-of-the-night-picnics" were common pastimes.

Today, it is impossible to get everyone together companywide: There are 17,000 employees in 12 states. The good times continue, however, with retiree dinners and programs, company golf and other outings, and company teams for almost every sport imaginable: bowling, softball, basketball, soccer, and flag football, to name a few.

Special events along with the daily work environment have fostered lasting employee friendships over the years. Many of the company's best and busiest people have skillfully blended workplace relations with conviviality and humor. Take Charlie Rudasill of Richmond, Virginia, who started in 1947 as a co-op employee. "One of my responsibilities was keeping the water cooler filled," he remembered. "I would walk across the street to the Rich Brown Brewery, where the bartender would spill enough beer in the cooler to fill it up, then bring it back to the office so the crews getting off in the afternoon would have something cold to drink." Of course, the company has never condoned such behavior, but then, Charlie has been retired for almost 20 years.

Early in his 24-year career, Michael "Mike the Spike" Barclay, an underground lineman in Kitty Hawk, North Carolina, would volunteer for all the jobs on Carova Beach. "We'd throw our surfboards up on the truck — one guy even made himself a little truck rack for his short board. After working hard all morning, we'd go surfing, fishing, or swimming during lunch," he said with a sly grin.

For Marlin "Mo" Patrick, an auger operator from Great Bridge, Virginia, remembering the practical jokes he played on employees over the years still makes him smile. "I used to have a supervisor who brought his lunch every day," he said. "He'd lock it in his truck, but when he wasn't looking, I'd open the back window, reach in, and take a bite out of his sandwich. Come lunchtime, he flew hot when he realized what had happened. He never did figure out it was me."

Like Patrick's recollections, William Bartlow's memories are also peppered with humor, and his "Work Hard, Play Hard" outlook probably sums it up for most Dominion employees: "It's not how it's dealt to you, it's how you deal with it," said Bartlow, a lead lineman from Charlottesville, Virginia, who started as a trainee in 1969. "A little fun never hurt anyone. But if you asked me what I'm proudest of, it's that anybody and everybody that works with me goes home in one piece every night. Nobody has been hurt on my watch that I know of. To me, that sums up my 40 years."

Even company executives lived by the "Work Hard, Play Hard" motto. On visits to Wall Street investors and analysts, "My dad, T. Justin Moore, Jr. [former chairman of VEPCO] must have had poles in his legs because he'd go to New York for the

ABOVE: The sluggers of VEPCO's 1931 South Richmond "Base Ball Team." Front row: H. L. Smith, J. D. Maxey, P. W. Dunkum, C. D. Grizzard, G. F. O'Brien, W. A. Bell, and Manager W. L. Baugh. Back row: J. W. Archer, E. R. Woodson, Captain J. P. Grizzard, L. T. Haddock, J. E. Lett, Walter Childrey, R. M. Haddock, P. J. Harris, and W. M. Wingfield.

RIGHT: The VEPCO Girls Softball Team in 1953 finished the season with 10 wins and 2 losses. Kneeling: Doris Viar and Lolene Hancock. Seated: Jackie Simpson, Naomi Green, Margaret Lawson, Carol O'Brien, and Shirley Eanes. Standing: Manager Jim Egan, Josephine Tyson, Coach Al Phillips, Marie Hare, Annabelle Lewis, Coach Joe Poleo, and Jean Williams.

"THE WHOLE TOWN TWINKLED"

Before electricity was widespread, postcards of brightly lit streets and buildings were popular. *ABOVE*: This card (undated) depicted the Virginia Light and Power Building in downtown Norfolk. VEPCO moved from there to Cromwell Road in 1952. *RIGHT*: (undated) The Virginia Railway and Power Company Building in Richmond at 7th and Franklin Streets was built "especially to be the headquarters of the Company ... it is of fireproof construction and stands highest in this respect in the state of Virginia." The exterior lamps around the fourth floor and the crown of torches were symbolic of the building's use. VEPCO moved from this location and into the current One James River Plaza at 7th and Cary Streets in 1978.

company and work 12 hours, then drag along everyone to dinner and then out for jazz," remembered Jay Moore, his son, a Richmond attorney. "It was this notion of 'We're all in this together, and we've got to work, but we're also going to find a way to have fun.' So they would hang out until midnight or 1 a.m., then get up by 7 the next morning ready for another full day."

AN "UNSEEN, UNSLEEPING PUBLIC SERVANT"

Electricity is no longer a newfangled luxury as in the trolley car days — it is an invisible force intrinsic to everyday life. The same can be said about Dominion Resources. For 100 years, Dominion has been unwavering in its commitment to supply customers with affordable, reliable electricity.

It has strived to live up to the role of an "unseen, unsleeping public servant" as referenced in the 1956 Annual Report.

For a company that sells a social and commercial necessity, being taken for granted is the ultimate compliment. Only when the lights go out do most customers give thought to the company "at the other end of the push-button," which is how one bill payer from the 1920s described his relationship with the company supplying his electricity. "When the power goes out or the gas stops flowing, nothing good happens," explains Thomas F. Farrell II, chairman, president, and CEO of Dominion. "Leaving aside the economic consequences, the disruptions to home life and the community are significant. That's why we try hard to be responsible. I would much rather pick up the paper every day and not see any articles at all about Dominion. We want people to be able just to say, 'I flip the switch, the lights come on, and the bill shows up at the end of the month.'"

Upholding public trust would be impossible without employees who feel an inherent sense of duty. Able to see beyond the long hours and tough work, they understand that what they do matters. It matters to the mother who needs her oven to prepare dinner for her family. It matters to the driver on the highway, dependent on streetlights to guide him safely home. It matters to the patient in the hospital, where conditions make energy necessary for life. And it hasn't just mattered in this age of hyper-customer service. This is a characteristic that company employees have embodied from the very beginning.

"I went to work one Friday at 8 a.m., and a storm came up, so the foreman put me on another crew," remembered John Thurston, a former supervisor of Construction who retired in 1986 after 40 years with the company. "I got off on Sunday at 6 p.m. and when I came home, lunchbox under my arm, my daddy said, 'Boy, where've you been?' I said I've been to work. And he said, 'Don't lie to me, nobody works for three days!' and [laughing], I said, 'Dang company I work for does!'"

Finishing the job with little fanfare, then promptly moving on to the next one, is what Dominion employees do best — and they do it with the utmost consideration for the customers they serve. It's called the "Dominion thing," a nickname coined by Kim Lowers, a manager in Suffolk, Virginia, who has been with the company for 24 years. "It doesn't matter who you are or where you are, when there is a job to be done, you step up to the plate and swing for a home run," said Lowers. "Regardless of the situation, we are all just trying to represent Dominion the best way we can."

Jack Holtzclaw, former VEPCO president, defined the trait very much the same way in 1932:

Be careful in the conduct of your part of the business, watchful of your every act as to its effect on the future, vigilant in maintaining the confidence of the public in our service, our aims and our citizenship, and we will probably be here after the smoke has cleared away to tell how the battle was won.

Indeed, Dominion is still here, and still making history … every day. ◆

The notion that a company's reputation rests on the character of its employees and how they treat customers has been around since the company's inception. Today, Dominion's Core Values — Safety, Ethics, Excellence, and One Dominion — reflect these early tenets. At right is one variation, VEPCO's Corporate Policy (also called "The VEPCO Creed"), printed in the *Current News* in 1970.

Virginia Electric and Power Company
Corporate Policy

Preamble

Public approval of any corporation depends on how well it understands and meets the present and future needs of its customers, on how well its management and employees provide the service to which the public is entitled, on how well it guarantees ability for future growth by preserving a fair return to its stockholders for the use of their money, on how well it conserves and utilizes the environment in which it operates, and on how well its policies, plans and programs are understood by its customers, employees, stockholders and the general public.

Policy

Therefore, it is the policy of Virginia Electric and Power Company:

TO EARN public confidence by providing dependable, courteous service of the highest quality at the lowest practicable cost and in a socially responsive manner;

TO EXERCISE leadership in anticipating and providing for the future needs of our consumers in a manner consistent with the environment;

TO MAINTAIN a record of productivity and profit that will assure our stockholders a fair return on their investment in order to enable the company to attract the capital essential to the future needs of our customers and the communities we serve;

TO PURSUE only those objectives that are consistent with the welfare of the public, willingly assuming our share of responsibility as a corporate citizen in the communities in which we operate, cooperating with our industry in research and development projects to solve problems that affect the public welfare, and observing the highest ethical and moral standards;

TO INSURE that each employee, in return for his or her diligence, is recognized as an individual entitled to dignity, respect, fair compensation, safe and efficient working conditions, and the opportunity for employment and advancement without regard to race, creed, color, religion or sex;

TO MAINTAIN open channels of communication for frank and consistent exchange of reliable information with our consumers, stockholders, employees, representatives of our government and the news media, and others who legitimately may have an interest in our operations;

FINALLY, as part of the largest single industry in our nation today, to so act and conduct our affairs that we demonstrate our faith and belief in the principles on which our Republic was founded.

John M. McGuinn
Vice Chairman & Chief Executive Officer

T. Justin Moore Jr.
President

Chairman, Board of Directors

ELECTRICITY DOES YOUR FARM WORK
Easier — cheaper — better

VIRGINIA ELECTRIC AND POWER COMPANY

VEPCo

VEPCO, the Virginia Agricultural Extension Service, and the Virginia Polytechnic Institute and State University (Virginia Tech) developed a working model of an electrified farm to promote the "Miracle of Electric Farming." Promotional literature for the traveling display read: "The greatest miracle of all is the way electricity has brought most of the good things of city life to the farm ... making farming more glamorous and attractive for today's farm youngsters."

CHAPTER 2

"Living Better — Electrically"

BEHIND EACH LIGHT is an unseen, unsleeping servant — electric power. Day and night it is on the job, serving home, business, and industry ... town and city ... suburb and farm. Electricity is the means to the easier, happier, more productive way of life and the demand for power is growing steadily.

1956 VEPCO ANNUAL REPORT

When the Virginia Electric and Power Company (VEPCO) was formed in 1925, its new name had a noticeable change: There was no reference to the company's longstanding transportation interests.

The transit business had been steadily veering off course since the early 1900s, with annual revenues sinking from $1,444,000 in 1910 to $290,000 in 1923 to a low of $85,000 in 1931. Bus service supplanting trolleys was partly to blame, but the automobile was another factor. No longer a fad, cars were becoming the main method of transportation for both city and country dwellers, and new roads financed from a gasoline tax under President Franklin D. Roosevelt's New Deal made it easier than ever for motorists to hit the highway.

The electricity business, on the other hand, was booming. The Roaring Twenties, a decade of social change and economic prosperity in America, was fueled by electricity. Although electricity had yet to become indispensable in rural areas, it was powering every facet of life. Improvements in electric motors increased the dependability and durability of everything from automobiles to appliances. Advancements in film, television, and radio technology transformed the United States into a mass-media society. Telephones — even transatlantic lines — connected the world in ways unimagined only a couple of decades before. And industries hummed along, thanks to better power transmission, increased electric usage in factories and offices, and new technologies that capitalized on electrical power. From 1900 to 1925, American electricity consumption grew 3,000 percent.

A COMPANY GROWS UP

The first few decades of the 1900s provided fertile ground for VEPCO to grow and flourish. Even during the Great Depression, service industries and utilities enjoyed solid growth and progress. VEPCO

A 1927 model kitchen in VEPCO's headquarters at 7th and Franklin Streets showcased the marvels of an all-electric kitchen and promoted the sales of new appliances.

was no exception, quickly acquiring several companies that expanded electrical service north into the Ashland-Fredericksburg areas of Virginia and south into Norfolk and eastern North Carolina. By 1930, VEPCO could tout 100,000 customers and electric revenues of $11 million. "Our business is rocking along and we are continuing to take VEPCO service to the highways and byways, and to make ourselves as valuable as we can as a business institution and as citizens of our States and communities," noted company president Jack G. Holtzclaw at the time.

New customers meant an increased need for dependable electricity, and VEPCO invested early in generating stations to keep up with the growing demand. As a result of the 1925 merger with Spotsylvania Power Company, the company boasted 14 generating stations serving 5,000 square miles. They didn't stop there. In 1927, the company completed its first major expansion at Norfolk's Reeves Avenue Power Station, making it the largest in the VEPCO system. With a load demand of 42,000 kilowatts, the Reeves Avenue Station was hailed as a state-of-the-art steam turbine-driven electric station, "where no moving parts are evident and the instruments are relied upon for the operation of this equipment."

In the decades that followed, VEPCO constructed two additional coal-fired generating stations in Virginia: Chesterfield Power Station in Chester in 1944, with a capacity of 50,000 kilowatts; and Possum Point in Dumfries, which went into operation in 1948 with a 60,000-kilowatt unit. The company's merger with Virginia Public Service Company in 1944 more than doubled the VEPCO service area and generating capacity by adding a series of systems in northern and western Virginia and in the Hampton Roads area near Norfolk.

SPREADING THE MESSAGE OF LIVING (AND FARMING) BETTER — ELECTRICALLY

Throughout company history, few positions, including that of CEO, have enjoyed as much visibility and status as VEPCO's home economists. In the early days of electricity, home economists provided crucial guidance in housekeeping and cooking using this new form of energy. "You have to remember that many of our clients were switching from coal, wood, and kerosene to electricity," said Nancy Woodlief, who started as a student trainee in the Home Services department in 1960. "Even experienced homemakers would look to us to help them understand their appliances and use them effectively and efficiently."

Cooking demonstrations were the most popular service offered, and the recipes created and distrib-

uted — such as Mexican Lunch and Cranberry Crunch — became family favorites throughout Virginia. Home economists also designed kitchen layouts, made house calls to demonstrate appliances, helped Girl Scouts earn cooking badges, assisted contractors with electrical plans for the entire house, and held workshops for civic and church groups. More importantly, they influenced decision makers — the homemakers. The forerunner to the Public Relations and Marketing departments (or today's External Affairs group), home economists were the company's public face. "It was all I ever wanted to be," said Susan Gardner, who began her career at VEPCO in 1965 as a home economist. VEPCO home economists "were in a class by themselves — all other home economist positions paled in comparison," she said.

Susan Gardner began working at VEPCO in 1965 as a home economist. "It was a job way beyond cooking," she said.

VEPCO's Home Services department often presented demonstrations to community groups such as the Girl Scouts. In 1951, a Virginia Beach, Virginia, Girl Scout troop participated in one of VEPCO's live window displays.

A 1966 VEPCO Home Services cookbook.

Besides teaching customers how to cook the "flameless easy way," VEPCO's Home Services department also dispensed marriage advice. Here, a Home Services representative, Miss Flickinger, encouraged young brides to learn how to cook in order to "hold their man."

RIGHT: Making the rounds of potluck dinners and church suppers throughout Virginia, Cranberry Crunch and Mexican Lunch were two of the most popular recipes from the VEPCO Home Services cookbook.

Their male counterparts in the agricultural sales and engineering programs, known as "Aggies," targeted a different demographic — farmers. They worked with 4-H and Future Farmers of America to acquaint students with innovative electric farming equipment and traveled to individual farms to convince established farmers of the benefit of "Farming Better — Electrically."

"When I started in 1951, people had only a small fuse box in their house to power their lights and refrigerator," remembered James Wellons, a former VEPCO agricultural representative who retired in 1989 after 48 years with the company. "We would work up a wire layout using a central meter pole in the yard so they could use electricity all over the farm. It wasn't too hard to convince them that electricity could help them with things like moving bales of hay on conveyors from the ground to the loft, or with drying greens after harvest." Wellons' counterparts on the commercial side would assist architects and engineers with complex designs for heating and cooling systems for large commercial projects.

Together, the efforts of these departments helped push electricity usage skyward, with residential electric usage almost doubling from 1955 to 1966. Recognizing that electricity had become a mainstay of everyday living, VEPCO disbanded the home economist programs in 1973

but continued its service to commercial and industrial customers through the work of service representatives and Area Development managers, the precursors to today's Economic Development group. Despite the demise of the home economists, Mexican Lunch and Cranberry Crunch can still be enjoyed at many a potluck supper. ■

Using an electric well pump and motor to distribute water around the farm was one of the ideas Jim Hamilton (*at left*) suggested to farmers in Virginia's Allegheny region about the benefits of "Farming Better — Electrically." Hamilton retired in 1994 after 62 years with the company.

Cranberry Crunch

1 cup uncooked quick cooking oatmeal
½ cup butter
½ cup all purpose flour
1 1-lb. can whole cranberry sauce
1 cup brown sugar

Preheat oven to 375 degrees.
Mix oatmeal, flour and brown sugar together. Cut in butter until mixture resembles coarse crumbs. Pack ½ of mixture in the bottom of a 1-½ quart baking dish. Spread cranberries on top of bottom layer. Top with remaining crumb mixture. Bake 25 minutes.

Mexican Lunch

1 1-lb. package pork sausage
1 cup diced onions
1 cup diced green pepper
2 cups canned tomatoes
1-¾ cup buttermilk
    or 2 cups sour cream
2 cups uncooked macaroni,
    shell or elbow
1 tablespoon sugar
1 teaspoon chili powder
1 teaspoon salt

Brown sausage, onion and green pepper in a large skillet. Add tomatoes, buttermilk, macaroni and seasonings. Mix thoroughly. Cover. Cook on medium high heat until steaming. Turn to low and simmer for 25 minutes.

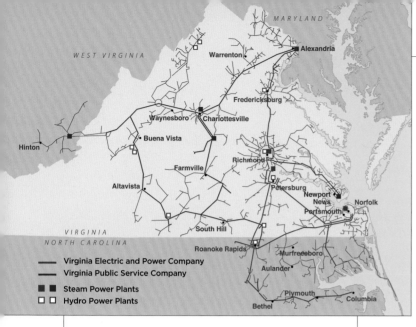

Virginia Electric and Power Company
Virginia Public Service Company
■ ■ Steam Power Plants
□ □ Hydro Power Plants

The company's service area doubled when Virginia Electric and Power Company merged with Virginia Public Service Company in 1944.

ELECTRICITY FOR ALL

In its infancy, electricity was a novelty. "Power was something we got from our mules, or by using our own muscles," remembered Floyd Yates, a Powhatan, Virginia, native born in 1903. "To think of electricity and all the little things we have today — why, you wouldn't have believed it."

Just as hard to believe were some of the audacious statements made about the miraculous properties of electricity. Quack doctors claimed it could cure most any disease, and at times they used electrical shock to treat rheumatism and other ailments. Nonsense aside, a 1934 article in *The Vepcovian* commented that:

> *Fifty years ago if someone had predicted that we would one day have electric refrigerators, ranges, hot water heaters, fans, and would sleep in a bed with an electric heating pad, he would have been considered a fool.*

It didn't take long, though, for the novelty to wear off and people to realize the "great blessing which electricity has brought to the human race."

Everyone wanted it. The question was, who would pay for it?

The issue had been debated since Theodore Roosevelt's presidency at the turn of the 20th century. The obvious answer was customers — but in rural areas, there were fewer customers to share the expense of installation. About $2,000, or $32,000 by 2009 standards, was needed to cover each mile of wires, poles, transformers, and labor. Private companies like VEPCO were hesitant to wait and recoup the cost as new customers were added; instead, they decided to charge large deposits and a higher kilowatt-per-hour rate to cover the fees upfront. These same private companies also held the common

ABOVE: On the back of an August 1945 electric bill, Reddy Kilowatt encouraged customers to can foods. *RIGHT*: Canning was promoted by VEPCO's Home Services department throughout World War II as a way to "increase vitality and physical fitness." VEPCO's model kitchens at headquarters and the local electricity offices often featured displays promoting canning.

belief that farmers had little use for electricity. Even so, VEPCO participated to some extent in early rural electrification efforts. In 1933, the company was recognized with the Martin Award, the highest prize in the industry, given to the electric company showing the greatest contribution to the advancement of rural electrification. Little more than six years later, VEPCO would be chastised for intervening in the progress of the Rural Electrification Administration (REA) — a flashpoint throughout Franklin D. Roosevelt's presidential tenure.

Roosevelt disagreed with the approach taken by private power companies. In his opinion, "The farmers above all should have … power, on reasonable terms, for cheap transportation, for lighting their homes, and for innumerable uses in the daily tasks on the farm." The debate intensified in 1936 when Congress passed the Rural Electrification Act to enact the REA's reforms. REA supporters argued that affordable electricity would drastically improve farmers' lives and productivity, and that the labor needed to implement the program would create much-needed jobs.

THE CREATION OF RURAL CO-OPS

As the Great Depression dragged on, the debate over public versus private power continued. The government had envisioned partnering with private power companies to electrify rural America, but the companies, including VEPCO, balked at the low price tag placed on accomplishing the feat. They also did not buy into the idea that low rates could turn a profit. Officials at the REA had no choice but to turn to farmer-run cooperatives to carry out the work.

Common in farming communities, cooperatives were formed by members who found it easier to pursue goals collectively rather than individually. In a surprisingly short time, Virginia's cooperatives mapped out a service proposal based on the location of members. The REA financed the projects, and the cooperatives constructed the lines. But private companies maintained an important role: They supplied power to the co-ops at the required wholesale rates. The plan worked. By 1939, about 20 percent of Virginia's farms had electricity — three times the number only four years earlier and more than any southern state except Texas and North Carolina.

Success, however, was tempered with tense relations. Private power companies eventually realized that electricity was just as valuable to rural customers. Even more, these areas could account for substantial income for electricity suppliers. It was inevitable that utilities would want to expand in areas typically left to co-ops, but the way they went about it was sometimes questionable. They challenged rate structures in court and used "spite lines" to connect wealthy service areas to the power grid while bypassing less-desired areas. One such plan backfired for VEPCO when the company sent a spite line through the middle of the Virginia Electric Cooperative's service area in Caroline County.

RIGHT: A 1932 electric bill from Petersburg, Virginia, recorded a $1.03 balance for the month. *BELOW*: Electricity was slow to reach rural areas, but three years after Roosevelt's Rural Electrification Act was passed in 1936, 20 percent of farms had electricity.

SAFETY FIRST

Safety. It's the one constant in 100 years of change at Dominion. As early as 1916, the company named "Safety First" as its standing motto, printing the proclamation prominently at the top of every *Public Service News* newsletter distributed on the company's early trolley cars.

In the same year, the company founded the General Safety Committee of the Virginia Railway and Power Company, the first of its kind created by a Virginia industrial organization. Its mission? "To spread the safety gospel by studying accidents and conducting a continuing campaign against their causes."

Throughout the last century, countless accident-prevention measures have been implemented for the sole purpose of keeping employees and customers safe. Early efforts included suggestion boards for posting employee-generated ideas, mechanical improvements in machinery, publicity to point out lax practices and common causes of accidents, and constant attention to avoiding carelessness. Contests designed to "lick old man accident" pitted departments against each other to boost accident prevention, and employees were encouraged to test their knowledge in periodic first-aid contests. A "Safety First" week began in 1916 and was held annually for years to stress that nearly every accident is avoidable, and that "the best safety device known is a careful man." As J.J. Hoard, a substation

RICHMOND SAFETY COUNCIL FLEET TROPHY

FOR THE BEST SAFETY RECORD IN FLEETS OPERATING MORE THAN 100,000 VEHICLE HOURS

AWARDED TO VIRGINIA ELECTRIC AND POWER COMPANY LIGHT AND POWER DEPARTMENT 1934

LEFT: Recognizing and rewarding safety have always been part of the company's culture. *ABOVE*: President W. E. Wood presented the 1929 VEPCO Girls First Aid Team with a congratulatory banner. *RIGHT*: A 1940 "Accident Elimination Contest" bulletin outlined the safety records for each division in the company. The bulletin also noted that VEPCO had won the national record over other electric companies for the third straight year.

foreman who retired in 1981 after almost 36 years, commented about working with electricity, "You don't make but one mistake."

Walter George, a safety manager who worked for the company for 38 years before retiring in 1984, helped identify and then write safety regulations for the company. "Automobile accidents were our biggest problem — and backing up the main culprit," said George. "We wrote and passed a rule that if two employees were in the car, one had to get out and help the other back up." Another rule targeted electrocutions, which generally occur from the shoulders to the fingertips. "We passed a rule that before you leave the ground, you put your rubber gloves and sleeves on. We felt we could eliminate 90 percent of the accidents, and over a

period of time, it paid dividends. It wasn't comfortable, particularly in hot weather for linemen, but neither was 4,000 volts when it hit you, either!"

Henry Poindexter, who worked most of his almost 36 years with the company in high voltage substations, said the company has always been extremely safety-conscious. "Some guys were working up a pole one time and they had 256 pieces of rubber goods up the pole," he said. "And the safety man wrote 'em up and said they didn't have enough! 256 pieces!"

Today, safety remains one of the company's four core values. Wearing appropriate protective clothing, eye wear, and hard hats is standard safety protocol. Meeting and exceeding safety guidelines set forth by the Occupational Safety and Health Administration (OSHA) is commonplace. "We go at

ABOVE: Demonstrations and mock drills performed throughout the company's history have helped employees save each other's lives in the field. These employees participated in the August 1986 Fire Safety Games at North Anna. *TOP RIGHT*: A 1988 lineman rescue demonstration.

a slower pace than we did 20 years ago when we were just trying to get something done," said Danny Allen, an electrician who began working at the Bremo Power Station in 1980. "It's because we're more safety-conscious now — if it means going slower to be safer, then that's what we do."

New and improved ways to be safer on the job are implemented as quickly as possible, with some processes culled from Dominion employees' own experiences. Employees like Dennis McDade even go so far as to create rap music videos paying homage to the value of safety:

> *... That's right, that's life, now you gotta*
> *play by the rules.*
> *Living dangerous ... are you trying to*
> *play the fool?*
> *I'm the reason why being safe is cool.*
> *Shiny hardhat, steel toe in my shoes,*
> *FR clothing, and my glasses approved ...*
> *I don't care what you gonna do*
> *But as long as you and your crew ... stay safe.*

Through heightened awareness, prevention, training, and accountability, Dominion's overall

safety performance has improved in recent years. Indeed, the hallmark of a well-managed operating company is low accident rates — an indicator that someone is paying close attention to business. "Safety has become more than a priority — it's a company value," explained Randy Sizemore, a senior safety specialist at Dominion's Innsbrook Technical Center. "Priorities change over time but values are constant."

At Dominion, the emphasis on safety starts at the top. "This is a hazardous business, and I don't want anyone getting hurt — not our customers, not our employees," said Thomas F. Farrell II, chairman, president and CEO. "We believe that every accident is preventable, that no injury is acceptable. And while our 'zero tolerance' approach has produced five consecutive years of improvement, our company will not be satisfied until we are accident-free. Our bottom line is this: When safety is compromised, everyone loses — employees, friends, families and our community." ■

Dennis McDade's "Safety Rap" has been a YouTube.com sensation, with more than 125,000 views. Electric companies across the country have used the video to kick off safety meetings and promote safety in a fun way. McDade (*far right*) made the video with fellow employees (*left to right*) Ashley Windsor, Norman Soaper, and Winton Funk.

LEFT: Throughout his tenure, VEPCO President Jack Holtzclaw personally presented service awards. Holtzclaw was president for 26 years, longer than any other president. In 1954, a year before he stepped down, he remarked, "I'm in a rut. I haven't had a promotion in 25 years."

BELOW: Vintage service award pins for 25 and 35 years of service.

Immediately, REA officials intervened and suspended all of VEPCO's work in the Commonwealth. "Encouraged" by the State Corporation Commission, VEPCO promptly changed its plans.

PUHCA'S SHAKE-UP

VEPCO's formation in 1925 was historic for reasons other than the company's newfound concentration on the electric market. That year also marked the beginning of the company's subsidiary relationship with Engineers Public Service Company. According to Holtzclaw, VEPCO's financial condition had been unsatisfactory before this relationship; it had been difficult to obtain necessary funds for needed expansions and improvements. Under the holding company, however, VEPCO flourished. "The change in the financial standing of the company

was remarkable, illustrating one of the most important, if not the most important phase of a holding company's usefulness to a subsidiary," the company president said. Holtzclaw believed the company eventually would have gone under without Engineers' intervention.

Once again, President Roosevelt disagreed. As part of his administration's "trust-busting," he demanded regulatory oversight of the 18 utility holding companies that controlled almost the entire utility industry. Holding companies served as a safety net for subsidiaries. They provided valuable financial, management, and engineering resources that individual companies, on their own, would not be able to afford. But holding companies also lacked consistent oversight from regulators since they usually operated across several states. With

such spotty oversight, the federal government concluded that holding companies were "frequently a menace to the investor or the consumer or both." In 1935, the Public Utility Holding Company Act (PUHCA) went into effect.

From the outset, VEPCO took a strong leadership position in fighting PUHCA. T. Justin Moore, the company's general counsel, had the responsibility — and honor — of presenting the industry's arguments before Congress. The holding companies lost "by just one vote in the Senate in a long, hard fight," remembered his son, T. Justin Moore, Jr., future VEPCO chairman. The elder Moore's tenacity and knowledge propelled him to the top of utility circles nationally and, in future years, he would "practically invent utility corporate law in Virginia, as well as some of the early part of the corporation code."

The passage of PUHCA cleared the way for the inevitable. In 1940, the government sued Engineers Public Service Company, requiring the divestiture of everything but VEPCO. Four years later, amid dissension from area cooperatives, VEPCO merged with the Virginia Public Service Company. With an increase of electric customers from 199,000 to 335,000, gas customers from 36,494 to 49,733, service growth area from 13,500 miles to 29,668 miles, generating capacity from 221,000 kilowatts to 339,250 kilowatts and employees from 3,943 to 5,301, VEPCO became one of the largest electric utilities in the United States.

Rather than keep VEPCO and divest its gas operations, as was required by PUHCA, Engineers Public Service Company dissolved. In July 1947, after 22 years as a large subsidiary of a holding company, VEPCO became an independent, publicly owned utility.

A TRUE ELECTRIC SERVANT

These massive regulatory changes, and the adaptations they required, unfolded against an ominous backdrop: America's entry into World War II. As defense efforts pushed the demand for electricity to an all-time high, VEPCO played a prominent role. Chesterfield Power Station was built expressly to power the Richmond-based DuPont and Reynolds companies, which produced chemicals and aluminum for the war effort. Reinforced concrete was used to construct Unit 1, rather than solid steel, because of the metals shortage. The company also provided power for other industries crucial to the military, such as munitions, explosives, uniforms, and medicine manufacturers, not to mention the farms where food for America's troops was grown. As noted in the company's 50-year history:

> VEPCO supplied the power for the war-crowded areas of Northern Virginia, swelled with the overflow of congested Washington; for the heavy industrial and U.S. Naval installations in Tidewater … the training camps like Fort Lee … the shipbuilding industry of Newport News … the Air Force base at Langley Field.

On the home front, VEPCO engaged in the company's first-ever efforts to encourage customers to conserve power for the war effort. A 1940s public service announcement featured Reddy Kilowatt, the industry's mascot, urging listeners to save energy:

> There's no shortage of electricity at the Virginia Electric and Power Company but Uncle Sam's asking everybody to conserve. Fuel, manpower, transportation and vital materials … all these things are needed to make electricity. Each little bit that you save, multiplied by thousands of other Americans, will be an important contribution to the government's volunteer conservation program. Help win the war by saving more!

The company's efforts did not go unnoticed. In 1946, the U.S. Navy commended the company and its employees "for meritorious service and outstanding performance rendered beyond normal responsibility during World War II."

When World War II ended, some analysts predicted a decline in demand for electricity. They assumed that the increase in power required by the war effort would naturally decline once the war was over. VEPCO even had anticipated selling the Chesterfield station under this same assumption. But utilities had underestimated the pent-up need for electricity by their residential consumers. On the contrary, electricity usage jumped 14 percent nationwide between 1946 and 1947. VEPCO's load growth rapidly reached record levels. "Never once was it dreamed by the officials and engineers of this company — or by the officials of the government — that such an unprecedented demand for service could possibly have come so rapidly," said Holtzclaw in 1950. A 1947 report forecasting usage for 1960 had already been exceeded in 1950, Holtzclaw elaborated, and the 1970 forecast was on its way to being woefully underestimated.

"Everybody wanted service after the war was over," remembered Vincent Sutphin, a 39-year veteran who started with the company in 1941 reading meters for 69 cents an hour. "If we had 20 service inquiries one day, we had 21 the next day to do. We never did catch up on our engineering work; we always had a backlog. It was amazing how we would scramble to get people service." As the suburbs mushroomed and new households proliferated, the company's number of electric customers increased by 50 percent in the 1950s. The idea of "Living Better Electrically" was becoming a way of life.

Gertrude Bullock from Accounting worked as hostess for the War Bonds and Stamps booth on the main floor of the Richmond office. As explained in *The Vepcovian* in 1942, "This is a war everybody is in. The kid in knee pants. The oldster with the cane. The housewife with the market basket. The white-collar worker. The blue-collar worker. The girl in the schoolroom. We're all in it."

THE PRICELESS COST OF ELECTRICITY

The immeasurable benefits of electricity are sometimes provided at immeasurable sacrifices. But few customers know how dangerous working with electricity can be. Many of the routine jobs throughout the Dominion workforce are extremely dangerous — even deadly — but potential danger is all in a day's work for the men and women who feel called to serve in a role that receives little recognition.

Of the 10 most dangerous jobs listed by the Bureau of Labor Statistics, two are performed daily at Dominion: drivers and electrical power line installers and repairers. Dozens of other positions companywide can be just as dangerous. Battling the weather, the physical nature of the job, and the perilous conditions that come from working around broken machinery ... these are a few of the reasons that "it's no work for sissies," as an early *Vepcovian* newsletter declared.

William Brooks from Norfolk remembered the day a fellow employee had a heart attack and fell over into a transformer. "It's bad enough to have a heart attack if you work in an office, but when you are working in precarious situations, it's even more dangerous," he said. "I know that safety is always emphasized by management, but it's reinforced even more with your guys on the line. We're like family. If one of us hurts, all of us hurt."

The sentiment is shared throughout the company. When three employees at Salem Harbor Power Station in Massachusetts were killed in 2007 by a steam pipe rupture, the grief was palpable throughout Dominion. "It was a painful reminder of the worst that can go wrong in an industrial workplace," said Thomas F. Farrell II. The company leader urged fellow employees to honor the fallen men by "doing everything you can to work safely today and every day."

In this 1970 photo by retiree Fred King, Norfolk linemen over the Elizabeth River worked on the bottom conductor from a hook ladder secured to the middle conductor above.

In 1963, G. R. Walker (*left*) saved the life of fellow North Carolina lineman Edward R. Gurganus (*right*). Walker cut the line and administered pole-top resuscitation. As a result, he received the Edison Electric Institute Resuscitation Award (*top*). The Latin inscription translates to "By the grace of God, through the hands of a fellow worker." The award was made of copper taken from the world's first light and power distribution system laid in 1882 in New York City by Thomas A. Edison.

Many improvements in safety over the years have decreased the risk of serious accidents and deaths. Obvious changes like wearing hard hats, ear protection, air-monitoring devices, and safety glasses — all optional in the past — are now mandatory. "Safety Days," today's version of the company's former "Safety Weeks," focus on safety deficiencies at various work locations to reinforce the safety message. Technological advances such as digital smart meters eliminate the need for meter readers to physically enter yards with dogs, fences, and overgrown bushes. Bucket trucks and "buck squeezes," the safety belts that keep linemen from sliding down utility poles, have reduced the number of accidents arising from pole climbing.

"Pre-job and post-job briefings, where supervisors review what and how a job is done, have helped tremendously," said Randy Sizemore, senior safety specialist for Fossil and Hydro Safety. "Human performance observations, where supervisors observe and critique performance, are another helpful tool, especially since most accidents are caused by human error. And our proactive *Safety Alerts* go out companywide to share information about accidents that almost caused an injury." In offices, small but effective measures target prevention, such as

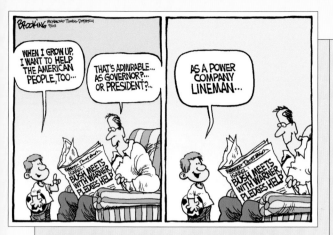

Richmond Times-Dispatch, September 24, 2003

training employees about the appropriate way to lift heavy files, keeping desk drawers closed to prevent falls, and discouraging employees from using handheld electronic devices while walking.

Environmental changes also have contributed dramatically to better safety for workers. "There's no way around it — coal plants are dirty places to work," said George O'Connell, a mechanic at North Branch Power Station in West Virginia with almost 30 years under his belt. "When I first started in 1980 at the Mt. Storm station, I couldn't see from one end to the other because of the noxious atmosphere. Today, there is just no comparison to what it was like back then."

And then there are the unexpected turns that even the most alert employee can't predict. "We were working just up from Duck, North Carolina, hooking up a home, and the trencher kicked up a few of these little 'dumdum bombs' apparently left over from World War II exercises," said Michael Barclay, an underground lineman with 24 years of service. "Another time, we were in a backyard full of all sorts of farm animals. My buddy bent over to tie his hooks onto his boots and a billy goat came out of nowhere and rammed him in the head. When I looked over, he was on his rear end across the yard with his hard-hat right down to his ears. Never saw it coming." ∎

The worst storm to hit Dominion's service area in its 100-year history, Hurricane Isabel caused catastrophic damage to electric lines and left 1.8 million people — 81 percent of customers — without electricity in 2003. Full service took two weeks to restore as workers from 18 utilities and 21 contracting firms — the largest workforce ever assembled by the company — labored around the clock. In the end, Dominion's storm restoration efforts cost $128 million.

THE LINEMAN

Up on the storm-swept cross arm,
Where the wind blows wild and free,
A cowhide belt and a chip of steel
'Twixt him and eternity.

When the thunder peals o'er the tree tops,
And lightning gleams on the hills,
It's then his work is awaiting him,
And he gets plenty of thrills.

When folks in houses cringe and shake
Before the storm has passed,
He handles death at his finger tips
To make the hot wires fast.

One slip of the hand and he's gone
To at least long days of pain,
But let him out and sure as sin
He'll be up on the poles again.

There's time he holds in his very hands
The life of a pal he loves,
And prays that he fails not in his trust
By a flaw in his rubber gloves.

But for all of that he's a common guy,
And very much carefree,
And he'll stick to you through everything,
The best pal you ever did see.

— Ernest Miller, 1932 *Vepcovian*

ABOVE: An ode to a lineman.
ABOVE RIGHT: A metal tag hammered into an electric pole just above ground level signifies the date of the pole's osmose test.
LEFT: After Hurricane Isabel, Dominion's mailroom was flooded with letters of gratitude from customers, such as this one from the Dooley family.

9-24-03

My power is on! You guys are an answer to my prayers. Thank you so very much for the hard work you have done. I have to tell you that my power went off on Thurs. at 5:50 PM. I had filled both tubs with water and one kitchen sink. We have a well, so I was trying to prepare in advance of the hurricane.

Upon completion in 1955, the Roanoke Rapids Dam in North Carolina was dedicated to former VEPCO President Jack G. Holtzclaw and his persistent effort in seeing the project to completion. Holtzclaw had died suddenly earlier the same year.

ABOVE LEFT: When the U.S. Supreme Court decision was announced on March 16, 1953, the Roanoke Rapids *Daily Herald* rushed a "Special Edition" to press the same afternoon. *LEFT*: The Roanoke Rapids Dam.

ANOTHER GOVERNMENT SPAT

VEPCO met the continuously growing demand for electricity with acquisitions and new power sources, including completion of the Roanoke Rapids Dam in North Carolina in 1955. Completion of the dam was the culmination of a long, bitter fight with the U.S. Department of the Interior. Twenty-two years earlier, VEPCO had gained approval from the Federal Power Commission to build a hydroelectric operation, and had even purchased all the land necessary to complete the project. But plans went on hold when the Depression struck. The availability of cheap coal and more efficient steam generation also contributed to the delay.

Then came the war. When it ended, the company's outlook was very different. Fuel costs had doubled and the VEPCO system was six times larger than it had been in 1929. The company reapplied for the hydropower license — and was denied. The U.S. Department of the Interior caused the ruckus, insisting that the Flood Control Act gave it complete responsibility for all future hydroelectric power supply. Among the government's arguments: The dam "will create a great hazard and may result in loss of life to children and others seeking recreation in the stream below Roanoke Rapids … sudden large discharges may carry off livestock watering in the streams … and the minimum release of 500 cubic feet per second will create shallow pools where fish may be taken without the sport of fishing." Walton Seymour, the chief of the Power Division at the Interior Department, even testified that it would be better if Roanoke Rapids were never developed than be developed by a private company.

The conflict escalated as a continuation of previous private versus public power struggles, rather than an environmental concern. After hearings before the Federal Power Commission and the lower courts, VEPCO took its case to the U.S. Supreme Court — and in 1953, it won. When the dam was completed in 1955, it was dedicated to Jack G. Holtzclaw, who had died earlier in the year, in honor of his 26-year presidency at VEPCO.

"COMPLETE ELECTRIC UTILIZATION"

Unbelievable as it seems today, VEPCO spent its first 50 years persuading and educating the public about the benefits of electricity. The logic was that as electricity usage increased, utilities would need to build newer, more productive power plants. New plants produced power at a lower cost, which would then be passed on to customers at a lower rate. And customers, using more power since it was less expensive, would generate the need for more power. This perpetual cycle seemingly satisfied everyone. "We were working with builders promoting what we called 'Gold Medallion Homes,' total electric homes," said Jim Poland, who retired as manager of community and government relations in the Norfolk division after a 38-year career. "We were not in the conservation mode; in those days, we were in a selling mode."

Advertisements boasted that "installing electric lights is as simple as rolling off a log." Electricity was credited for transforming everyday chores into "push-button housekeeping." One ad even suggested that electricity helps a woman stay young.

Regardless of their exaggerated claims, the ads paid off. By 1959, the idea of "complete electric utilization" had been realized, with "housewives … finding new leisure and pleasure through such appliances as vacuum cleaners, washing machines, refrigerators, and electric ranges." It was the Golden Age for electricity, a time when the rigors of everyday life were eased or eliminated by its power, a time when rates, driven by consumer demand, remained stable or decreased 42 times from 1926 to 1969 — figures unheard of in today's marketplace.

Strong market conditions helped VEPCO evolve from a collection of companies into a major force in the utility industry. Revenues increased from $2 million in 1909 to $135 million in 1959, with 18 generating stations working to meet the demand for power. The first 50 years had been bright, but there was "no halt in the steady, forward motion of progress." As the company reflected on its golden anniversary: "If there is a lesson to be learned from history of these 50 years it is this: In a free and competitive economy the force of forward motion is constant, and the future can — and will — surpass the past. Our goal? To make life easier, more productive, and happier for all." ◆

ABOVE: A doorbell featuring the "Total Electric Gold Medallion Home" certification. *RIGHT*: Throughout the 1960s, VEPCO continued to promote the inexpensive, convenient luxury of electricity.

It Only Costs Pennies…
To Sleep in _COOL_ Luxury!

Will _YOUR_ New Home Have _AUTOMATIC_ Drive?

VIRGINIA ELECTRIC and POWER COMPANY

VIRGINIA NATURAL GAS

Dominion's 100-year history would be incomplete without the story of Virginia Natural Gas (VNG), whose history stretches back 160 years. The two companies have an interwoven past that intersects at various dates and moves forward in parallel before eventually taking different paths. "In the beginning, natural gas was a very small part of a large entity," said Lee Starkey, retired public and media relations manager. "As VEPCO grew, the interplay between the electric and gas industries became more apparent. Although we were independent, we were always part of the big picture, a blended part of the whole."

STAKING A CLAIM

VEPCO's foray into the gas business began on July 1, 1911, when all of the properties, rights, franchises, and other assets of the Norfolk and Portsmouth Traction Company were transferred to the Virginia Railway and Power Company. After that, VEPCO's gas division played a supporting but essential role in company business, an issue addressed in a 1931 *Vepcovian* newsletter:

> *The progress of the gas department has not been rapid, but it has been steady, even in these trying times. It has always done a good job, but it has been somewhat like the fellow who did his work well and quietly....*

Although electricity dominated the marketplace, the company's gas operations grew steadily, serving 60,508 customers in 1950. A year later, pipelines transported natural gas to the gas plants in Norfolk and Newport News for the first time. Almost overnight, revenues doubled, and by 1955, gas operations accounted for 7 percent of VEPCO's revenues and exceeded $7 million annually. Gas distribution also grew, from 1.7 billion cubic feet in 1951 to 3 billion cubic feet in 1953, an increase of 75 percent.

LEFT: Virginia Natural Gas executives Gene Keeling (*kneeling*), Jerry Causey (*left*), and Bill Fritsche (*right*) were instrumental in the company's success. *BELOW*: VNG lapel pin.

ABOVE: Wrapping a newly welded steel gas main was all in a day's work for employees in Norfolk in 1955. *RIGHT*: Coal and coke, still transported by mules in the 1920s, were rendered into manufactured gas at "purifying plants" like this one on Monticello Avenue in Norfolk.

SURVIVING THE SEVENTIES

Utilities suffered greatly in the 1970s, and gas companies were particularly hard hit due to a 1954 U.S. Supreme Court ruling that authorized the Federal Power Commission to regulate gas prices at the wellhead. Doing so allowed the Commission to set prices for gas crossing state lines. Consequently, producers chose to sell within their state jurisdiction, where higher prices could be obtained. Over the next 20 years, interstate gas production plummeted, creating natural gas shortages and an increase in prices just as the Middle East oil embargo hit.

In 1973, VEPCO's gas division added only 248 new customers, bringing the total customers served to 125,525. In 1974, the Virginia State Corporation Commission placed a statewide moratorium on connecting new natural gas customers; the total number dropped to 124,395. Four years later, Congress finally enacted the Natural Gas Policy Act to end price controls on wellhead gas — only after interstate transmission suppliers had imposed drastic curtailments that decreased VEPCO's gas customer count to 119,298.

A 1931 billboard in Norfolk touted the ease of heating your home with natural gas.

ABOVE RIGHT: A 1970s advertisement advised customers on how to conserve energy.

INDEPENDENCE DAY

Having survived the prior decade, VEPCO began the 1980s with its gas and electric operations intermingled. However, president William W. "Bill" Berry, a proponent of competition, believed that the growing availability of natural gas would allow VEPCO's gas division to operate more successfully if separated from VEPCO. On October 2, 1981, VEPCO's gas division was renamed Virginia Natural Gas (VNG) and became an independent operation. That independence was fully realized in 1986 when Dominion Resources, VEPCO's parent company, made VNG a separate, wholly owned subsidiary.

VNG's independence, however, was short-lived. In 1990, Consolidated Natural Gas (CNG) purchased VNG, recognizing the opportunity for expansion of natural gas services in one of the fastest-growing areas in the nation. At the time, VNG was achieving record customer growth with a service territory from the Hampton Roads area into central Virginia and plans for a new intrastate pipeline in northern Virginia. "For the most part this change of ownership will be transparent to our employees and customers," said VNG president William F. Fritsche, Jr., at the time. "We will continue to be a separate company, Virginia Natural Gas, with the same operating facilities we have now."

When Dominion merged with CNG in 2000, VNG was reunited briefly with its former parent company before being sold, under State Corporation Commission rules, to AGL Resources, Inc., an Atlanta-based energy holding company. ■

The Virginia Natural Gas name, coupled with the signature blue-and-white flame logo, became well-known throughout the Tidewater area of Virginia.

Chesterfield Power Station, the largest fossil fuel station in Virginia, has been a workhorse for Dominion. When rumors of war swirled in the late 1930s, VEPCO predicted additional generating capacity would be needed soon. Plans to expand Richmond's 12th Street Station were scrapped when studies indicated that the existing generating equipment would require total replacement with more modern units. An expansion of Norfolk's Reeves Avenue Station was also considered, but the War Production Board argued for a less vulnerable location. Ultimately, the current 300-acre site on the James River in Chester was chosen. Placed into service in 1944, Unit 1 was a coal-fired, tandem-compound, hydrogen-cooled turbine generator with a net capacity of 63,500 kilowatts, an initial pressure of 850, and a heat rate efficiency of 12,000 BTU/kWh. By contrast, Unit 6, which began operation in 1969, is approximately 9,600 BTU/kWh — a 20 percent improvement over those 25 years, which is significant. Shown is an aerial view of the 1949 expansion.
BOTTOM: The cover of a 1948 Pathfinder magazine featured the million-dollar generator "quietly staffed by six men."

10 Cents

March 10, 1948

Pathfinder

NEWS MAGAZINE

Volume 55   Number 5

New Million-Dollar Generator

More Power for U. S.

Becoming Dominion

Times couldn't have been better for Virginia Electric and Power Company (VEPCO) when the second half of the 20th century rolled around. Electricity was cheap — so cheap that while the cost of living rose 126 percent from 1941 to 1967, the cost of electricity dropped 44 percent. Some industry experts even predicted that electricity eventually would become too cheap to meter.

These were the "golden years" for utilities, when regulatory intervention from state and federal government was minimal, and customers and investors were typically satisfied with their utility service. Specifically, VEPCO was enjoying a reputation as one of America's most respected utility companies. With 60 years of unprecedented growth, it was clear that the stability and predictability of the regulated, traditional business model for utilities was serving the company well.

The 1960s saw a steady increase in customers, a continued decline in electricity prices, and phenomenal economic growth. Toward the end of the decade, the company witnessed 14 percent-per-year growth spurts as a result of rapid population and industrial growth in its service area. In 1968 alone, VEPCO authorized three major construction projects in an effort to meet demand: a third addition to the Mt. Storm mine-mouth station, a second nuclear generating station at North Anna, and the construction of a pumped-storage facility in Virginia's Marble Valley, later moved to Bath County when the site was deemed unsuitable by geologists. The company also began installing underground electric distribution lines for residential customers, a move that later became standard protocol for newly developed residential areas. It was a year that surpassed all others in events that would shape the future of the company, remarked John M. McGurn, VEPCO's president and CEO at the time.

Dominion purchased Cove Point, one of America's largest liquefied natural gas (LNG) facilities, in 2002. Coincidentally, the Maryland plant was originally constructed through a partnership between Columbia Gas System and Consolidated Natural Gas (CNG), which merged with Dominion in 2000.

Who, then, could have guessed that in coming decades, the landscape of the utility industry would change forever? "There was a period of calm before the storm in the late 1960s and early 1970s," said T. Justin Moore, Jr., then VEPCO's president and CEO, in a 1985 interview. "Rates were still dropping, and we were being praised for our shift away from coal to oil. We were voted Utility of the Year in 1971 by *The EL&P (Electric Light & Power) Gazette*."

In 1971, *The EL&P (Electric Light & Power) Gazette* presented VEPCO with the Electric Utility Award of Excellence. The award was given annually to the most outstanding utility in the nation. *From left to right*: T. Justin Moore, Jr., VEPCO president; Robert A. Lincicome, editorial director of the magazine; Parm Pritchard, publisher of the magazine; and John M. McGurn, VEPCO chairman and CEO.

A TURN-ABOUT FOR RATES

Change was brought about by several economic factors, but in the end, it centered on one contentious issue: rates. In 1970, the company asked the Virginia State Corporation Commission for its first base rate increase in 10 years.

As the decade dawned, so, too, did rampant inflation, increased fuel prices, oil shortages, and expanded licensing and regulatory procedures, including stricter environmental regulations under the new National Environmental Policy Act. The federal government reacted by raising interest rates to fight inflation, which backfired. Most businesses cut back on expansions, but VEPCO and other utilities in the midst of aggressive nuclear construction projects didn't have that option. The company's ambitious capital expansion programs simply grew more costly. "We wish the news was good, but that's rarely the case these days," said Moore in a 1971 open letter to employees.

The dismal outlook grew into a full-blown storm with the Middle East oil embargo of 1973–1974, in which Saudi Arabia and some other Middle East nations stopped exporting gas and oil to the United States for political reasons. In those days, VEPCO promoted electricity usage — not conservation — and, like other utilities, had come to expect that the continual increase in demand, coupled with new technologies, would push prices lower. Neither happened in 1974, when sales decreased for the first time since World War II.

The news kept getting worse — so much so that one analyst commented in *The Wall Street Journal* that "it's as if they have a jinx or something." VEPCO's "financial pickle," so called by then-president Stanley Ragone, was worsened by ill-timed coal-to-oil conversions. In the late 1960s, when oil was plentiful and inexpensive, it made sense to build oil-fired units and convert existing units from coal to oil to combat the shortage and soaring prices of coal. When the oil embargo hit, that logic collapsed. VEPCO was especially vulnerable since, with the conversions, oil accounted for 60 percent of the company's power generation.

"It seemed like a great idea at the time," said James T. Rhodes, VEPCO's CEO and president from 1989 to 1997. "Oil was more environmentally friendly and very cheap compared to coal. And because most of our coal stations were on rivers, it was easier for us to barge in oil than it was for other utility companies located inland."

VEPCO had no choice but to request a series of base rate increases that were higher than the rate of inflation to offset the bleak financial situation. "Rate increases arouse your customers, alienate your friends, and activate your enemies," remarked Moore at the time. "No businessman in his right mind asks for that kind of trouble if there is any way to avoid it."

The State Corporation Commission sets the rates that customers pay for electricity. "When I came to work in 1966, if we added a customer or sold more electricity, the rates went down because of the efficiency of scale," explained Paul Hilton, senior vice president-Regulation. "It would always reduce unit cost when we built a new power plant so it was easy to reduce rates — there's no effort in that."

Increasing base rates is more complicated. "It's a very complex and deep process with months and months of paperwork, audits, and disagreements," said Hilton. "There is give-and-take between the company and the Commission." Throughout the 1970s, VEPCO submitted five requests for base rate increases.

VEPCO wasn't alone in this crisis. In metropolitan New York City, for example, Consolidated Edison dealt with the fallout from the oil embargo

What do you say to your customers when you have to increase prices?

When someone raises the price of lemons, someone else has to pay more for lemonade.

And no matter how much you value your customers—and no matter how much you hate to increase their expenses—if you're in charge of the lemonade stand, you have to raise your prices. You may not like it, but

that's inflation.

It's that way with electricity. Prices for the fuels needed to generate electricity are still climbing, and nobody in Virginia has to buy more of those fuels than Vepco. Add to that the rising costs of financing and constructing new power plants, and you've got the inevitable. Price increases.

Conservation really does help. And Vepco will continue to fight for a reliable and affordable supply of electricity. We'll continue to point out the need for construction of new power plants as long as the need is there. And we'll continue to strive for a reliable, economical and balanced use of fuels.

Of course, that doesn't mean

those unwanted increases will just go away. But it does mean they'll be kept as low as possible.

And in these inflationary times, that in itself is some encouragement.

Vepco

Rate increases in the 1970s sparked widespread criticism of VEPCO, and the "lemonade campaign," which was lambasted throughout the state, didn't help. In 1978, protestors mocked the company by setting up a lemonade stand similar to one depicted in a VEPCO advertising campaign. The demonstration took place downtown in an empty parking lot across from the original VEPCO headquarters building. Other customers created petitions to block the rate request, saying that VEPCO should work on cutting back its own expenses before asking its customers to pay higher electric rates.

in part by eliminating its stock dividend in 1973. Because utility stocks were (and are) regarded as relatively sound "widow-and-orphan" investments, the move was a shock not just to Con Ed shareholders but to national financial markets. It signaled that the utility industry was in deep trouble.

Rate increases are never popular, but with the economy suffering as it was in the 1970s, the news incensed the public further, and confidence in their utility companies plummeted. "The price of oil doubled, and that, of course, caused the price of fuel to double for the company," said Bill Berry,

THEN AND NOW: ALL IN A DAY'S WORK

Gone are the days of climbing creosote poles, using computers that required an entire floor, and keypunching payroll cards. Today, efficiency, safety concerns, and advances in technology have contributed to many of the changes in the way work gets done at Dominion. But regardless of the era, the honor and challenge of providing a vital public service to customers remains unchanged.

1947 The highest operating voltage was 115,000 volts and the company's system was connected only to Carolina Power and Light (now Progress Energy). All of the design work was performed using slide rules and manually produced design drawings. Lines had to be removed from service for maintenance and repair. Electro-mechanical devices controlled the circuit breakers that protected the system.

2009 "Our extensive 500,000-volt Extra High Voltage transmission system is interconnected to all neighboring utilities. Computer-Aided Design and Drafting systems have replaced manual design and drafting, and we deploy computer technology through Supervisory Control and Data Acquisition and for control of circuit breakers. Many maintenance tasks are performed 'barehand,' allowing lines to remain in service."

David Roop, *director, Electric Transmission Operations*

These men patrolled 480 miles of transmission lines by truck from Quantico, Virginia, to Elizabeth City, North Carolina, in 1933. *From left to right*: J.C. Hurst, J.D. Hill, G.R. Henry, R.A. Will, C.E. Benton, C. Herron, Harry Frisbie, M.J. Briggs, W.H. Heintzman, superintendent transmission lines; A.R. Jolly, assistant superintendent; J. Johnson; and M.S. Epperson. Today, 6,000 miles of power lines are patrolled annually using helicopters loaded with so much specialized equipment — infrared, LiDAR, and other high-definition cameras — that only the pilot and one person can ride. A typical 10-hour day yields about 7 hours of flight time and covers 150 miles of transmission lines.

1947 "I hand-delivered bills — it was more economical than to mail them at three cents apiece. All we delivered were bills just folded over, and I'd stick them in the customers' doors. In a big apartment complex I could do as many as a thousand a day. I actually covered a lot more territory than a meter reader did. I developed some pretty powerful legs back then."

Tom Jarvis, *retired vice president of Regulation*

2009 eBill service was created in May, 1999 as a free service so that customers could receive, review, and pay their electric bill electronically. In December of the same year, 5,320 accounts were enrolled. In 2009, 453,423 electric accounts, or 18.89 percent of Dominion's 2,400,537 customer base, are paid online.

1951 "We used to dig holes by hand. Using a nine-foot spade, we'd dig down six-and-a-half feet and then dig the dirt out by hand. We'd do that all day until we got the poles set and started building the lines. There was a name for the men who worked on the ground: 'grunts,' because we did a lot of gruntin'!"

Charles Ellison, *Petersburg, retired director of operations*

2009 "Today, we use a truck that has a boom and an auger drill attachment that both digs the hole and sets the pole. In simple terms, the labor of the 'grunt' work has been mechanized."

Rodney Blevins, *vice president, Distribution*

In 1960, the company purchased 10 time-saving Polecats, or hydraulic diggers, at a cost of $19,000 each.

1955 "The System Operators Office monitors telemetering instruments that electronically show power generation at all major generating stations, along with the amount of power required by customers. The console, about the size of an electric range, can instantly accelerate the production of electricity at generator turbines a hundred miles away."

The Vepcovian, November 1955

2009 The System Operations Center monitors tens of thousands of data points from all over the transmission system and beyond using a state-of-the-art Energy Management System that runs on computers the size of a pizza box. The EMS provides tools that automatically analyze the data and present the operators with useful information about the current state of the grid. The generation dispatch signals originate from a regional control center in Valley Forge, Pennsylvania, and are relayed to the generators by the EMS via secure, high-speed data networks.

System Operator J. B. Korte worked at a new computer in the System Operations Center (SOC) in 1959. The SOC also included a map board measuring 6 feet by 14 feet.

Clayton Beale (*left*) and Sammie Black serve on today's 63-employee SOC team. Monitoring devices include computers and a map board measuring 18 feet by 108 feet.

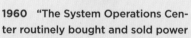
1955 "Meter readers walk nine to twelve miles a day and read as many as 600 meters. The job may require crawling underneath houses, climbing into attics, and scuttling up crude ladders at construction sites in order to read the meter."

The Vepcovian, August 1955

2009 "Smart meters" transmit meter readings electronically and offer customers more control over electric bills. The innovative model program opens doors to a wide range of energy conservation options.

1960 "The System Operations Center routinely bought and sold power across our state borders, but the only participants in the power markets were integrated utilities. There weren't many players in the market."

Harold Adams, *project director in the generation business development group*

2009 "Dominion Virginia Power is a member of PJM Interconnection, which operates a competitive regional wholesale electricity market encompassing all or parts of 13 states and the District of Columbia. PJM has 500 members, including integrated utilities, independent generators, retail electric suppliers, and energy traders."

Harold Adams

1963 The completely "transistorized" IBM 1401 computer eliminated long and complicated clerical work. Rate revisions, which previously took 80 hours to enter, were computed in the "almost unbelievable" time of 21 minutes. "The company used 1401 computers that occupied an entire floor. With a whopping 64K of memory, they could run one job at a time." In 1970, the company upgraded to the IBM 360, better known as the "Red Baron," so named for its red door panels. It was the first of its kind to be installed by a utility.

Bill Mistr, retired senior vice president, Dominion Capital

2009 "More than half of Dominion's employees use personal computers with an average memory thousands of times greater (2 GB) than the early versions of mainframe computers. Current mainframe computers have even more memory (40 GB) and process data in near 'real' time with no wait time. Use of space is now about the size of an office desk."

Jim Claypoole, project director, IT Risk Operations

In 1971, it took four people between 160 and 200 hours to complete — *by hand* — the 8,000 IRS W-2 Wage and Tax Statements sent to employees by VEPCO. Dixie Bryant, currently an employee for 50-plus years, was surrounded by boxes of W-2 forms. In 2010, employees could download and print their own W-2s at their desks.

Supervisor W. C. "Buck" Schermerhorn looked over the company's new state-of-the-art IBM 1401 computer in 1963: the card-read punch (*left*), processor (*center*), and printer (*right*). With 64 kilobytes of memory, the computer revolutionized clerical work. By contrast, a modern 12-gigabyte thumb drive can hold up to 12,200 times more data. *ABOVE*: Data was entered by means of punch cards.

1964 "All of the bookkeeping was done by hand. Our typing was on a manual typewriter. We used to have to fight to use the mimeograph machine! And when we got our first Xerox machine, it was like, gee! It was one of those wet paper [jobs], where you had to run it through the water. That was really something to behold for us — that we could get away from that mimeograph machine."

Anna Brooks, retired senior customer service representative

2009 "Today, our financial statements are based on up-to-the-minute 'real-time' processing. We also have the ability to drill down, meaning that we can see via computer all information about a particular account. The fact that our system can 'talk' to other systems consolidates our efforts."

Pat Vines, director, Financial Analysis and Planning

1972 "Whenever we needed to lower a motor into a hole at a power station, we'd hook a crane to straps around the motor, then climb on top to guide it down into the hole."

Randy Sizemore, senior safety specialist

2009 "There's no way we'd do that today! We still use the crane and straps, but now we guide the motor into the hole by hooking a tagline to the straps and working beside the motor as it lowers into the hole."

Randy Sizemore

DOMINION'S FIRST CENTURY

1952 Like most utilities, the company focused its political involvement on "encroaching socialism." Ads appeared periodically in newspapers throughout the VEPCO service area, along with Annual Reports that warned customers and employees of the dangers of hidden socialism. One said: "There's one clue that will help you recognize this hidden socialism. It's the old line: 'Let the federal government do it — or run it — or take it over — or own and operate it.' When you hear that, look out. For the more things the federal government runs, the closer we are to socialism — whether we want it or not — and the fewer rights and freedoms we have left for ourselves."

2010 Dominion formally established a Political Action Committee (PAC) in 1979, with 227 employees participating. The group's mission has stayed constant, as its 2009 brochure explained: "Politics is not a spectator sport — raise your voice! [Our] effectiveness as a pro-business political advocacy force depends on voluntary involvement from all our companies." The PAC made contributions totaling $1,078,265 and had 1,708 members in 2009. Dominion also maintains an External Affairs unit, which advocates on behalf of the company in state legislatures and at the federal level.

1973 "[As a lineman,] you climbed up the pole around 8:30 in the morning and didn't come down until lunchtime — you stayed on the pole. And then you'd go back up and stay on the pole 'til 3:00 or 3:30. The bruises on my legs stayed for three years after I stopped climbing poles."

John Croslin, *retired superintendent and safety supervisor*

2009 "Today, we use fall protection like a Buck Squeeze at all times, and we still use climbing hooks strapped around our shoes and legs. We also wear gloves: work gloves if we're only going up the pole, and rubber gloves and sleeves for energizing. Our poles are salt-treated, which makes them harder and cleaner. The old creosote poles were extremely dirty and they'd cause burns. And lifting jib cranes make our job a little easier — before we'd have to carry our materials up with us."

Doug Brown, *safety performance advisor and 39-year employee*

1982 "The Telecommunications department began when we shifted from old wireline rotary switching Chesapeake & Potomac Telephone Company equipment to computerized Private Branch Exchanges, or PBXs, purchased, constructed, and maintained in-house. We also went from a mobile radio system with simplex single channel to multiplexed communications channels with computer screens mounted in all field service equipment. That department grew from three original members to 165 engineers and technicians by 1983."

Calvin "Cal" Lucy, *retired supervisor of Administrative Services – Telecommunications*

2009 Dominion's fiber network is at the heart of today's communications. The move began when the Telecommunications department eliminated leased circuits to save money. (That department became part of Information Technology in the early 1990s.) Since then, the company has installed 1,340 route miles of fiber, most of which is overhead optical ground wire. All commercial operations offices enjoy wide area network and local area network connectivity with extremely high reliability.

LEFT: Practicing overhead distribution work in the 1970s were Virginia trainees (*left to right*) David McHaffey, Hampton; Keith Wooldridge, Williamsburg; and Wayne Lambert, Hampton.
BELOW: Lineman Gregory Smith at Dominion's training facility in Chester, Virginia, in 2008.

VEPCO's then chairman, president, and CEO. "It put us in a bind, but it also put our customers in a bind. And when oil doubled yet again, we really began to get lambasted with criticism."

"WELCOME TO VIRGINIA: OWNED AND OPERATED BY VEPCO"

Almost overnight, VEPCO went from an admired and favored utility to a scapegoat for anyone with a gripe about the country's financial straits. Meter readers, linemen, and other employees driving company cars were forced off the road by angry drivers shouting obscenities out the windows. They were cornered at grocery stores and parties by friends who wanted to know why their bills had gone up. Even their spouses and families were heckled. "It was just awful," remembered Susan Gardner, a retiree who began her career at VEPCO in 1965 as a home economist. "People had always loved the home economists but suddenly everyone was livid about their electric bills and they took it out on us. It got to the point where I dreaded going to church. I'd get there at the last minute and leave as soon as it was over." Being the target of such negativity was personally painful for employees

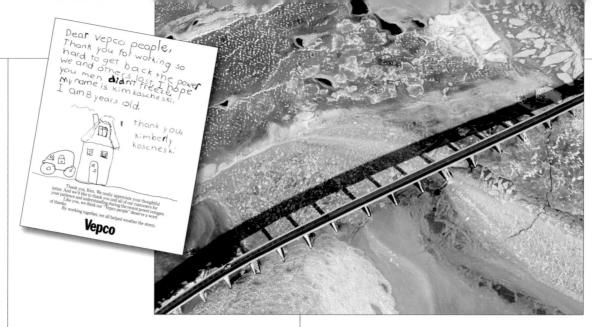

who, until now, had been held in high regard for doing a job that improved the lives of others.

The political backlash was equally vicious, with politicians — particularly "Howling" Henry Howell, a three-time unsuccessful Virginia gubernatorial candidate — whipping constituents into a frenzy over VEPCO's rate increases. Bumper stickers and signs plastered across the state displayed slogans like "Keep the Big Boys Honest," "VEPCO: Very Expensive Power Company," and "Welcome to Virginia: Owned and Operated by VEPCO." One 1979 article in *The Wall Street Journal* even referred to VEPCO as among the worst-run companies in the nation.

"When the oil embargo hit, we were horrified," remembered Bill "Reddy Kilowatt" Crump, the company's former chief lobbyist. "Oil prices went through the ceiling and

"Howling" Henry Howell was a fiery populist and one of the most vociferous opponents of VEPCO in the 1970s. In his 1973 gubernatorial race, he used VEPCO as a whipping boy for everything he considered wrong in corporate America.

ABOVE: The harsh winter of 1977 — so cold that parts of Chesapeake Bay froze over — created an especially heavy demand for power. *LEFT:* At least one customer was happy with VEPCO's quick response to getting the power back on after the freeze. A letter by young Kim Koscheski, used in a 1978 ad, said "I hope you men didn't freeze."

that meant our capital projects were going through the ceiling and everybody was just raising Cain."

UNDER THE WEATHER

As if company woes weren't bad enough, the winter of 1977 was so cold that much of the James River and parts of the Chesapeake Bay froze over. Water needed to generate steam to produce electricity was unavailable. And units needed to replace those out of operation for weather-related reasons were off-line themselves for repair.

As the demand for electricity increased, the company was forced to implement a series of rolling blackouts that prevented any one area from being without power for more than a few hours. It was the first time in VEPCO's history that the company couldn't provide enough power to meet demand. "We rotated power to people's homes,"

explained Berry. "It was a terrible thing to have to do in the dead of winter, and the newspapers blasted us for it. The only thing I can say is that it went as smoothly as something as unpleasant as that could go."

A HOLD ON NUCLEAR

Simultaneous to VEPCO's turmoil was the diminishing confidence in nuclear power by the end of the 1970s. Increased construction and financing costs drove the national average capital costs per kilowatt from $150 in 1971 to more than $600 in 1976. Likewise, public concern over safety began to heighten. In February 1979, Surry Unit 2 was removed from service for replacement of its steam generators. In March 1979, the Nuclear Regulatory Commission (NRC) ordered several nuclear units, including both at Surry, to be shut down (Unit 1) or remain shut down (Unit 2) until their ability to withstand a severe earthquake could be demonstrated.

Surry Unit 1 returned to service in October 1979. The earthquake reanalysis for Surry Unit 2 was completed while it was shut down for the steam generator replacement. Unit 2 did not return to operation until 1980.

On March 28, 1979, the accident at the Three Mile Island nuclear station near Harrisburg, Pennsylvania, dealt a severe blow to the entire national nuclear program. Only a year before, nuclear performance nationwide had been the best ever, and the NRC had just about finalized its guidelines for nuclear waste disposal sites. Then the repercussions of Three Mile Island ushered in moratoriums on issuing new nuclear licenses, rigorous regulatory requirements, and maintenance disruptions that affected generating capabilities during periods of heavy electricity usage.

As the old way of doing business in the utility industry was vanishing, VEPCO remained perhaps too comfortable in its traditional role. The company was slow to recognize the changing economic climate. Moreover, management, assuming that other forms of energy would eventually be phased out, had poured its financial and operational resources into the nuclear program, neglecting the fossil fuel operations to the point it was using "patch-and-run" maintenance.

"Our plan had been to add more nuclear units," explained Harold Adams, project director in the generation business development group. "We had four units planned at Surry, four for North Anna, and were even dreaming of four more at another location. Then the economy turned south and Three Mile Island caused a wave of new regulations for nuclear. … The subsequent delays financially strapped the company."

VEPCO had already started building North Anna Unit 3, but eventually deconstructed the unit and scrapped plans for Unit 4 altogether after briefly considering converting the two to coal generation. Although the State Corporation Commission disallowed return on equity for these expenditures, the company was ultimately able to recover its costs. A *Washington Post* editorial in 1979 commented:

> *VEPCO's original decision to begin North Anna 4 was right at the time it was made. But since then the whole development of the economy has*

ABOVE: One James River Plaza, VEPCO's future headquarters, shown under construction in 1977. LEFT: During the energy crisis, VEPCO, like other utilities, promoted President Nixon's "Project Independence," which called for energy independence. Nixon said, "Let this be our national goal: At the end of this decade, in the year 1980, the United States will not be dependent on any other country for the energy we need to provide our jobs, to heat our homes, and to keep our transportation moving."

> *shifted and the decision to cancel the plant is the right one now. Utilities all over the country face similar decisions. It's important not to penalize them for making the unconventional choices that will ultimately save the customers far more than they cost.*

Nuclear capacity, however, continued to be an important asset. In 1984, the company was one of the few utilities to reduce rates, mainly due to its reliance on nuclear energy. Customers were paying

VEPCO began producing a community calendar in the early 1980s to provide customers with "at your fingertips" information in the event of a nuclear emergency. An ongoing practice, in 2009 the calendars were distributed to 72,000 households within a 10-mile radius of the North Anna and Surry power stations in Virginia. Customers near Kewaunee, Wisconsin, also receive an informational calendar, while customers near Millstone, Connecticut, are given a booklet. Shown is a 1993 calendar that featured Virginia folk artists.

Tours at the visitor centers at Surry (*station shown in background and 1967 sketch at left*) and North Anna power stations educate the public about the importance of nuclear energy. The centers' exhibits include models demonstrating how electricity is made from atoms and the energy's path from uranium mines to home light switches, as well as hands-on experiments with open and closed circuits and interactive displays that allow guests to create electricity using their own body's energy. In 2009, 5,795 people, including school groups from the area, visited the centers.

2 percent less on average than a year earlier. It seemed that the company had gotten out of the expensive business of nuclear construction just in time. Not until 2002 — almost 25 years later — did the company reconsider adding new nuclear units to its generation fleet.

SHORING UP THE COMPANY

The tumultuous 1970s were spent putting out fires; the 1980s signaled a time of regrouping. Little could be done about rate increases; they were as "inevitable and about as welcome as death and taxes," said a 1981 VEPCO *Currents* newsletter article. When Berry began his tenure as VEPCO's chief executive in 1980, he vowed to keep them below the rate of inflation. It was a promise he kept. Just as impressive is that despite the economic woes of the 1970s, Dominion continued to pay dividends on its common stock throughout the decade. In fact, the company has never missed a payment since it began paying dividends in 1925.

At the same time that VEPCO was backtracking from its nuclear construction projects, it also was getting out of the more costly oil-fueled power business. The oil-to-coal reconversion program — one of the industry's largest — commenced in 1979 and was completed in a record five years.

The benefits were immediate. The reconversion reduced the company's imported oil consumption by 20 million barrels a year, lowered fuel charges for customers, and triggered new and improved operating efficiencies. This fulfilled what CEO Moore had described as "a shift from emphasis on construction to an emphasis on operations — getting the greatest possible output and efficiency from our existing units."

BECOMING DOMINION

The company's leaders have a long history of viewing the industry landscape not only to the horizon, but beyond. Bill Berry certainly did so. With a unique vision for the future, he began talking about the idea of competition and deregulation as early as 1981. His concept suggested that generating stations compete through a bidding process for buyers, an idea made feasible by the Public Utility Regulatory Policies Act (PURPA) passed by Congress in 1978. PURPA was designed to promote the efficient use of energy, but it also created opportunities for businesses other than utilities to produce electricity.

Charismatic and well-liked at all levels in the company, President and Chief Operating Officer Jack Ferguson had a "Let's get things done" attitude. He worked tirelessly to transform VEPCO's operations into a "well-oiled machine," laying groundwork for efficiencies that continue and have been enhanced at Dominion today.

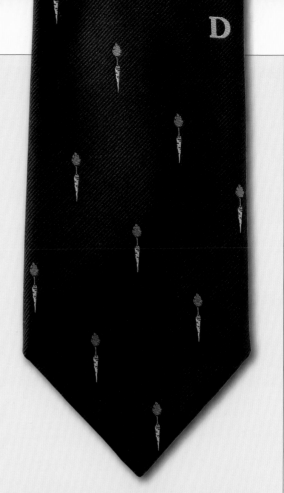

CEO Bill Berry started the "Carrot Club," VEPCO's first management incentive program, in 1981. Though he cut top management's salaries by 10 percent, Berry promised full salary restoration plus bonuses if the company's bottom line improved. As Bob Rigsby, a former VEPCO president, remembered, "Bill wanted to create camaraderie, so he handed out ties, money clips, and belt buckles, all with a carrot theme. He and Tom Capps even had pants appliquéd with carrots." The incentive program was eventually institutionalized and expanded to include all employees with earnings tied to the company's financial performance.

Former VEPCO CEO Bill Berry testified several times at Congressional hearings about the benefits of competition in the utility sector. When Berry first shared his views at an industry meeting, he came home and told his wife, "I was in a room with a few hundred people and the only ones who agreed with me were a PhD from MIT, a lawyer from the Environmental Defense Fund, and a New York regulator. And if they agreed with me, I must be wrong."

"Over time, a strong minority of supporters organized within the industry," Munsey explained. "Aided by strong supporters in the U.S. Department of Energy and the Federal Energy Regulatory Commission, that group worked on the necessary legislative and regulatory changes. Bill testified several times before Congress and kept up the pressure. Other executives nationwide joined the campaign and played important roles, but Bill was the most prominent. It was an exciting time for all of us, because we felt we were doing something of lasting importance for the industry and our country."

Although still unsure of the shape that any free-market changes might ultimately take, Dominion executives began to prepare. (They were realistic about the length of time such changes would require, and indeed the legislation Berry championed ultimately took 11 years to pass in Virginia.) In that period, the company began to reshape itself by forming Dominion Resources, Inc. On May 19, 1983, VEPCO was merged into Dominion as a wholly owned subsidiary. At that time, three shares of VEPCO common stock were surrendered for two shares of Dominion common stock, a two-for-three reverse split of VEPCO into Dominion.

Berry theorized that competition between utilities and independent power producers would make companies more efficient and save consumers money with less expensive electricity. He "believed that he could no longer risk investors' money in huge projects under a regulatory regime that might not allow him to get that money back," Hilton said.

When Berry went public with his views in a 1981 speech to the Edison Electric Institute in New York, the reaction by his peers was "underwhelming." "I felt like a skunk at the garden party," he remembered. Everard "Ev" Munsey, then vice president-Public Policy, recalls how controversial and upsetting this approach was for the entire industry. "It was a huge change from the traditional way the industry had operated," he emphasized. "The idea of competition in some parts of the electric industry had been broached by academics, but Bill was the first executive to embrace it and spell out the practical aspects." Electric co-ops and

other providers that relied heavily on government subsidies were particularly fearful, as were some state regulators who feared a loss of control.

Berry proposed dividing electric utilities into three components: generation, transmission, and retail distribution. Only the latter should be considered a natural monopoly, he said. In doing so, each would have greater flexibility, efficiency, innovation, and increased management specialization. VEPCO, which was already buying cheap coal-fired power from adjacent utilities near Midwestern coal fields, saw firsthand the advantages of a freer market in bulk power.

Over the next few years, Dominion added several nonregulated subsidiaries: Dominion Capital, Inc., a financial services company; Dominion Lands, Inc., to oversee the company's land holdings and invest in real estate and property development; and Dominion Energy, formed to capitalize on the flourishing cogeneration market and later, to acquire and develop natural gas reserves. During the same period, the company undertook a process to "rebrand" VEPCO as Virginia Power and spun off its gas division into a separate utility — Virginia Natural Gas.

After Dominion Resources was formed in 1983, the company set to work cleaning up its public image with new names and logos. "We had two considerations," remembered former CEO Bill Berry. "We wanted to get away from 'VEPCO: Very Expensive Power Company,' and we knew that people in North Carolina didn't like to pay a company with 'Virginia' in the name."

and the new look is being shaped by the forces of competition," he declared in a 1988 *PowerLine* magazine article.

When the bidding was over, Dominion had signed contracts for 19 projects providing 2,086 megawatts — enough to power more than two million additional households.

Gary Edwards, director-Cogeneration Services, and his team reviewed bids from companies seeking to provide 1,750 megawatts of new generating capacity. In all, the company's first competitive bidding process in 1988 produced offers totaling 14,000 megawatts of capacity — eight times more than requested. A specially designed data processing system was created to cope with the huge number of variables. By 1999 Dominion had signed 80 contracts representing 4,400 megawatts. Today, the portfolio has more than 30 contracts representing 1,861 megawatts; the difference is a result of contract buyouts and plant purchase programs.

TESTING THE WATERS OF COMPETITION

The notion of "power purchase ideology," a fancy term for purchasing power rather than generating it, was the company's solution to the shortage of electricity created from VEPCO's cancellation of its two nuclear units. In the four years prior, Virginia Power had experienced a 31 percent growth in retail sales. But modern times called for an emphasis on transmission rather than generation, with the company expanding its role to include energy management.

"Berry asked me to shop around and see if we could purchase power," remembered John "Bucky" Oates, a retired executive vice president. "They generated it; we brought it in. It was complicated — and it worked — but it was a significant change in philosophy. It was counter to the traditional idea that utilities had to build enough generation to take care of their own customers."

On June 1, 1988, company vice president Larry Ellis showed up at work to find a conference room crammed with dozens of packing crates filled with thousands of pages of documents — all from outside suppliers willing to provide new generating capacity to the company. It was evident that the largest and most complex purchase of generating capacity yet made under competitive bidding was a success. "No one had ever conducted a capacity bidding program on anything approaching this scale," said Ellis at the time. "We had to create our own evaluation system from scratch to judge a broad spectrum of highly innovated and creative proposals effectively. We even had to design completely new data processing techniques to cope with the huge number of variables involved." Berry's vision for competition had finally come to fruition. "The electric utility industry is getting a facelift,

THE DOWNSIDE OF COMPETITION

The move toward a more competitive utility market-place happened at a volatile time. Three factors were at play. First, President Ronald Reagan and federal lawmakers aggressively advocated deregulation in major industries; the most notable example was the 1984 breakup of AT&T, America's only major telephone company for generations, into regional "Baby Bells." Second, the economic downturn of the 1970s persisted, with unemployment rates nudging into double digits into the early 1980s. Last but certainly not least, the 1980s ushered in a heretofore unheard-of computer age. Previously only extremely large companies had used computers, usually mainframes. When smaller systems became available, many companies invested in technology for the first time. These first-generation technologies were not cheap. But advances in technology were streamlining how business was conducted — and who was conducting it. It simply didn't take as many people to do the same jobs as it once had.

As a result of all these factors, companies across all business sectors aggressively cut costs and staffs. Words such as downsizing, right-sizing, and reengineering entered the American lexicon. The utility industry was no exception. Anticipating a competitive marketplace, and understanding that excess would not be tolerated in any area of operation, Dominion undertook the first layoffs in its history, eliminating almost 3,000 positions between 1989 and 1994.

"It was known as the 'June Prune,'" remembered Dixie Bryant, a payroll supervisor who has worked for the company for 50 years. "When I first started, the feeling was that if you go to work for VEPCO and do a good job, you'd have that job

Competition in the marketplace required that Dominion streamline operations for optimal efficiency. Throughout the 1980s, the company promoted the idea of employees working smarter and more efficiently, as evidenced in this 1984 poster. Today, the same work ethic is encouraged through Dominion's Six Sigma program.

until you retired. But 1989 was the beginning of a change in culture, and in order to survive and be the strong company we are today, it had to happen. And it was happening all over. VEPCO and Dominion have always treated employees with care, respect, and dignity, and even in the layoffs, I feel they were generous with the severance packages."

Some employees were moved to different departments; early retirement and severance packages were

other options. In all, 21 percent of the workforce was cut. "This is a painful yet necessary step in our effort to reduce costs and prepare for competition," said Rhodes, who was president at the time. "We are steadily making progress toward our goal of becoming a leader in the 'new' electric utility industry, but achieving that goal means that we have to make some hard decisions and that, unfortunately, means good employees will lose their jobs."

"THE GREAT UNPLEASANTNESS"

Painful as the layoffs were, nothing compared to the company's self-inflicted wounds caused by differences of opinion in how the company — as a whole — should position itself for the 21st century.

In 1994, Dominion's management moved to change the makeup of Virginia Power's board of directors. Consolidating duplicate operating entities, similar to efforts Dominion had made in recent years by combining the financial and legal functions of Virginia Power with its own, was proposed in the name of efficiency. Efficient or not, Virginia Power's leadership disagreed.

The dispute mushroomed into a public debate about the larger, more fundamental issue of corporate governance. Who gets to elect the company's board and management: the subsidiary, Virginia Power, which at that time accounted for more than ninety percent of Dominion's total revenue, or the parent company, Dominion Resources, which owned one hundred percent of Virginia Power's stock?

Nobody questioned whether parent companies, structurally, have final authority in business matters. Rather, this unique disagreement centered on the sincerely held beliefs by all parties that the company's most promising intellectual capital resided in their respective boards. Virginia Power had made tremendous strides since the strife of the late 1970s and had emerged as one of the nation's finest utilities — the big kid on the block. The Dominion parent company was the newer kid on the block, but had proven itself an innovative, fast-moving player just as the nation's traditional utility sector began its move into diversification, deregulation, and free markets.

The dispute led to intervention by the Virginia State Corporation Commission, which regulates utilities. The SCC was concerned that the conflict could affect the operations of the subsidiary utility.

It was an important issue not only for Virginia Power and Dominion, but also for the Commonwealth of Virginia. While the Virginia State Corpo-

The August 17, 1994 headline in the *Richmond Times-Dispatch* reported that a settlement between Dominion Resources and its subsidiary, Virginia Power, had been reached pending approval from the State Corporation Commission. In doing so, the boards of both entities were reorganized with several board members sitting on both Virginia Power and Dominion Resources boards.

ration Commission had direct supervision authority over Virginia Power, it did not have the same control over Dominion. "It was a very critical point in Virginia corporate history," said Robert "Bob" Burrus, Dominion's attorney throughout the crisis.

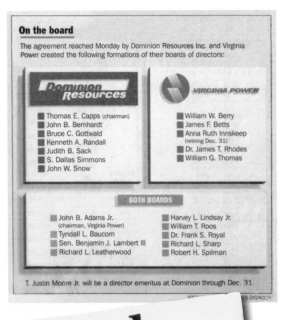

On the board

The agreement reached Monday by Dominion Resources Inc. and Virginia Power created the following formations of their boards of directors:

Dominion Resources
- Thomas E. Capps (chairman)
- John B. Bernhardt
- Bruce C. Gottwald
- Kenneth A. Randall
- Judith B. Sack
- S. Dallas Simmons
- John W. Snow

Virginia Power
- William W. Berry
- James F. Betts
- Anna Ruth Innskeep (retiring Dec. 31)
- Dr. James T. Rhodes
- William G. Thomas

BOTH BOARDS
- John B. Adams Jr. (chairman, Virginia Power)
- Tyndall L. Baucom
- Sen. Benjamin J. Lambert III
- Richard L. Leatherwood
- Harvey L. Lindsay Jr.
- William T. Roos
- Dr. Frank S. Royal
- Richard L. Sharp
- Robert H. Spilman

T. Justin Moore Jr. will be a director emeritus at Dominion through Dec. 31.

Tension between the two sides had been building for some time. The regulated Virginia Power business recognized its strength and history in the utility industry along with a strong sense of public mission; it pushed for continued efficiencies where little risk was involved. Dominion, the holding company, was charting new territory with no boundaries on the nonregulated side of the business. It realized the untapped potential of diversification.

Perspectives and agendas differed, and the only commonality was shareholder interests. "We called it the 'great unpleasantness,'" said Tom Chewning, former executive vice president and CFO for Dominion. "Looking back, I can see a lack of understanding and appreciation probably on both sides for what the other was doing. The people on the nonregulated side felt like the people in the regulated business didn't have enough entrepreneurial spirit. And the people on the regulated side looked at the nonregulated business as being undisciplined and not conservative enough. It was very disheartening and very disturbing, and it certainly interrupted what we had going on. The distraction kept us from concentrating on what we should have been doing."

The parent company, Dominion, ultimately prevailed in a decision that would broaden the company's corporate vision and reinforce its obligation to serve both customers and shareholders. "If you avoid conflict it doesn't resolve anything," Chewning said. "At the end of the day, the outcome was clear so that people on both sides could move on to a new day."

The decision was a turning point that would propel Dominion's future success, but not one without consequences. While the legal wrangling between sides lasted about 18 months, the bitterness from the "feud" lingered for years.

Settlement of feud awaits SCC blessing

BY MICHAEL MARTZ
TIMES-DISPATCH STAFF WRITER

The blessing of state regulators was the last hurdle remaining yesterday on the path to peace between Virginia Power and Dominion Resources Inc., its parent company.

The Richmond-based companies asked the State Corporation Commission to end an investigation into the dispute that erupted publicly two months ago over management of the

spokesman Mark G. Lazenby.

Everette G. Allen Jr., a lawyer for Virginia Power, said, "The healing process not only has begun, it's progressed a long way."

COMPANIES

Wall Street reacted positively to the settlement announcement. Dominion's stock closed up 50 cents a share at $38 on the New York Stock Exchange. A rally in the bond market also helped utility stocks.

The company's major shareholders also were pleased by the end of

owns 4 million Dominion shares.

The SCC began the probe on June 17 to determine whether Dominion had violated a 1986 order governing the relationship between the holding company and Virginia Power, the state's largest public utility.

The dismissal request related only to the portions of the investigation dealing with "corporate governance" issues, such as the degree of independence that the SCC can require of Virginia Power's board without harming the ownership rights of Dominion shareholders.

In a joint statement yesterday, the companies said: "We have estab-companies said: "We have estab-

In 1993, Dominion expanded its service area by acquiring a generating plant in Argentina, followed by facilities in Belize, Bolivia (*shown here*), Peru, and the United Kingdom. These assets were sold less than 10 years later.

DEREGULATION: A NEW DIRECTION

Dominion Resources was well-positioned for a more competitive electric industry; it had been laying the groundwork since 1983, when the company first began diversifying its business interests. "There were people in the industry who wanted to see utilities do new and different things," said Eva Teig Hardy, former executive vice president of Public Policy & Corporate Communications. "In the 1990s we were trying to think through what was going to happen. It really was a transformative period in the industry."

On the regulated side, Virginia Power had emerged as an efficient, low-cost producer with a fundamentally sound service area. By 1996, the company owned and operated nuclear, coal, natural gas, oil, and hydroelectric generating stations that served two million residences and businesses in a 30,000-square-mile region. The company was also proactive when federal law created new opportunities for bulk transactions in wholesale power, tripling sales and working with five times as many trading partners than before.

Dominion's nonutility operations also were blossoming. For several years, Dominion worked to diversify from its core utilities operations. Dominion Capital complemented its debt and equity investments by venturing into the commercial and mortgage lending businesses and commercial real estate development. Dominion Energy plunged into the foreign energy market with the 1993 purchase of a 98-megawatt generating plant in southwest Argentina. Its ownership and operating interests quickly grew to 27 generating facilities in six American states, Argentina, Belize, Bolivia, and Peru, and 460 billion cubic feet of proven reserves throughout several major gas-producing regions of the United States. In 1995, the company acquired a new subsidiary: East Midlands Electricity, one of the strongest electric distribution and supply companies in the United Kingdom.

These acquisitions were engineered by Tom Capps, the company's chairman, president and CEO at the time, who also foresaw competition and deregulation as the future of the utility business. "Capps had an incredible vision, but he realized that in order to provide services more efficiently in a less regulated environment, several critical acquisitions needed to be made so that a deregulated company would be able to supply customers with energy regardless of what happened in the marketplace," said attorney Burrus. "His judgment proved very much correct, and because the assets he acquired were worth a lot of money, he made it possible for the company to change direction yet again if needed."

In the end, the timing couldn't have been better for deregulation. Like his predecessor, Bill Berry, Capps predicted that competition would penetrate the retail side of the industry. "But it will come differently than it came to the airline, transportation, banking, natural gas, and telephone industries," Capps said. "In those industries, competition was virtually created by the stroke of a pen at the federal level. We think that in our industry, each state will set ground rules reflecting its view of the public interest."

That's exactly what happened. In 1999, Virginia Governor Jim Gilmore signed into law legislation establishing a detailed plan to restructure the electric utility industry in Virginia. The plan called for deregulation of generation by 2002, when customers would have the right to choose their energy supplier. Across the country, 14 states approved retail choice for customers the same year, and eight opened gas markets to competition.

To meet requirements for deregulation, Dominion agreed to operate its generation activities separate from its transmission, distribution, and retail operations in 1999. Virginia Power retained its name for the transmission and distribution company under state regulation. Both regulated utility and merchant nuclear, hydroelectric, and fossil fuel stations were brought under the management of Dominion Generation.

A CONSOLIDATED COMPANY, FOUR MILLION CUSTOMERS STRONG

Although Dominion's international acquisitions were primarily profit generators, they also served as intensive tutorials about doing business in a deregulated market. "We actually bought East Midlands in England partly to figure out how it was all going to work," said Tom Farrell, who joined the company that year. After 18 months, Dominion sold East Midlands, making $647 million that helped fund a share buyback program and pursue other investment opportunities. In 1999, the company sold its Latin American interests in a strategic shift toward a concentration on the energy-intensive Northeast,

mid-Atlantic, and Midwest regions of the United States, referred to as "MAIN to Maine."

Unloading the foreign businesses was a savvy move that favorably positioned the company for an unprecedented merger. In 2000, Dominion purchased Consolidated Natural Gas in a deal that boosted the customer base to four million in five states across the mid-Atlantic, Northeast, and Midwest. As required by the Public Utility Holding Company Act as a condition of the merger, the company sold its portfolio of financial services at

Dominion Capital and used proceeds to pay down debt and reinvest in the focused energy business. These steps transformed Dominion into one of the country's largest gas and electric utilities, and provided competitive muscle for emerging deregulation.

"It was a bases-loaded home run for the company," said William "Bill" Mistr, senior vice president of Dominion Capital, who headed up the merger team. "What most people don't understand is that it was more than combining two companies — it was combining several since Dominion was operating

When the U.S. was beginning to deregulate energy in 1997, Dominion devised a strategy for competition. It ultimately decided to focus on one of two new markets, New England, rather than also trying to compete in California. After acquiring Kincaid Power Station near Springfield, Illinois, the name "MAIN to Maine" was coined for the market area. It equals the world's second largest economy, with 121 million residents consuming 40 percent of America's energy.

Dominion
D
January 31, 2000

as three separate entities at the time. Everyone had their own turf, and it was a huge undertaking to convince everyone to relinquish control and consolidate operations. It was about setting expectations and then getting everybody on board. ... It was about change management."

In the same year, Dominion purchased Northeast Utilities' Millstone power complex in Connecticut, adding two operating nuclear reactors to its fleet. It was fitting that Dominion mark the consolidation by bringing the entire company together under a recognizable, unifying brand name: "Dominion," with subsidiaries adding "Dominion" as a prefix to their existing names.

Because of Dominion's ability to adapt, a critical trait for all successful enterprises, the merger was recognized by the *Financial Times* as the industry's most successful change in strategic direction. The need to change had forced the company almost 50 years earlier to reconsider its stance in the marketplace; that reflection led to VEPCO's strategic merger with Virginia Public Service. Now, in the new millennium, the ability to adapt ultimately would set Dominion on a course for future success. ◆

Dominion's merger with Consolidated Natural Gas closed after business hours on January 28, 2000. Members of management rang the closing bell following the first day of trading for the newly merged Dominion. *From left*: Richard Grasso, New York Stock Exchange Chairman; Tom Capps, president and CEO of Dominion; George Davidson, new Dominion chairman and former CEO of Consolidated Natural Gas; Tom Farrell, president and CEO of Dominion Energy; Patty Wilkerson, Dominion vice president and corporate secretary; Tom Chewning, Dominion senior vice president and CFO; and Dave Heavenridge, president and CEO of Dominion Capital. *RIGHT*: After the merger, Dominion adopted a new logo.

THE HISTORY OF CONSOLIDATED NATURAL GAS

An old adage, "two are better than one," rings especially true regarding Dominion's merger with Consolidated Natural Gas (CNG). When the final papers were signed on January 28, 2000, Dominion became the nation's largest fully integrated natural gas and electric company, with combined annual revenues totaling $8.6 billion and assets exceeding $24 billion.

And to think it all started with one man's dreams of retirement. In 1998, George Davidson, former chairman and president of CNG, announced his pending retirement after 11 years at the company. "Little changes like that always catch the interest of

The history of Consolidated Natural Gas (CNG) began in the late 1800s when industrialist and visionary John D. Rockefeller (*left*) founded Standard Oil Company. He appointed pipeline-builder Calvin N. Payne (*right*) to oversee the company's natural gas business. When the Public Utility Holding Company Act of 1935 required holding companies to divest their public utility subsidiaries, Standard Oil first fought the order but eventually spun off CNG as an independent, fully integrated natural gas company. *ABOVE RIGHT*: This commemorative poster celebrated the company's 50th anniversary.

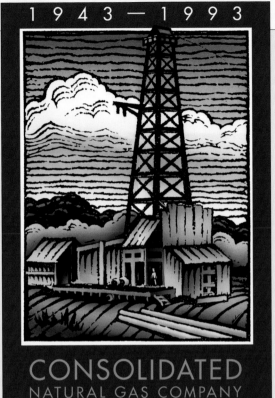

1943 — 1993

CONSOLIDATED
NATURAL GAS COMPANY

other companies interested in a merger or acquisition," said Davidson, who soon found himself meeting with several interested companies. "I sat down with four major players: Dominion Resources, a natural gas company like ours, and two gas and electric companies. After a year or so of meetings, it was clear that Dominion was the best partner for us. Our cultures and values were similar, and Dominion really didn't have any natural gas assets other than some production in the Appalachian area. It just made sense that the two would complement each other."

After the merger was announced, CNG received an offer $2 a share higher. Davidson refused the offer but was immediately sued by shareholders. "There are thousands of stories of how this went down to the wire, but I really felt in the long run that Dominion was the better deal," explains Davidson. "That played out for awhile, but eventually, we proved it."

The merger brought together two strong companies with equally compelling legacies. Just as Dominion's family tree has roots stretching back to

the infancy of the fledgling electricity business, the history of Consolidated Natural Gas can be traced to the creation of the natural gas business.

In the late 1800s, John D. Rockefeller was looking for a way to grow his vast empire of Standard Oil Company beyond refineries and into exploration and production. But rather than hitting black gold, South Penn Oil Company, a subsidiary, discovered large quantities of natural gas in West Virginia. Initially, Rockefeller wasn't interested; natural gas was considered more of a problem than an asset because of its high combustibility. Often, the gas would simply be burned off in the oil fields. But a determined employee, Daniel O'Day, convinced him otherwise. Rockefeller tapped Calvin N. Payne, an innovative pipeline builder, to "pursue the gas business earnestly," an edict Payne took seriously.

The original Hastings Station was built in Wetzel County, West Virginia, in the early 1900s. It consisted of two 4,500-horsepower compressors — the largest engines ever used to pump natural gas at the time. It was the hub of the company's natural gas operations, with gas collected from production areas, processed, and pumped to markets in Cleveland, Ohio, and Pittsburgh, Pennsylvania. Hastings was also one of the first extraction plants where by-products such as propane, butane, and natural gasoline were extracted, separated, and sold. Expanded and modernized many times, Hastings remains a hub where Dominion processes natural gas and pumps it to market.

WORLDS DEEPEST WELL HOPE NATURAL GAS CO. MARTHA GOFF. 4190.

In 1916, Hope Natural Gas Company broke a world record by drilling to a depth of 7,386 feet on the Martha O. Goff farm in Harrison County, West Virginia. The well exceeded the existing deepest well in Germany by 37 feet. The project was commenced with the idea of testing for deeper oil and gas horizons in West Virginia than what had been previously encountered.

lease owner. In 1965, the company formed its present interstate pipeline system by merging its two principal pipeline companies, Hope and New York State Natural Gas. Five years later, CNG acquired West Ohio Gas Company in Lima, Ohio, adding another 50,000 customers to its utility franchise.

Throughout its history, CNG has answered problems with innovation. When deliveries of gas fell below contract volumes and the first restrictions were placed on new residential hookups in the 1970s, the company responded with several ambitious supply initiatives: the establishment of CNG Producing Company; a project to import and re-gasify

The 1937 construction of New York State Natural Gas's Line No. 8 in Tioga, Pennsylvania.

For the next 30 years, Standard formed, merged with, and acquired companies to explore for gas throughout the Appalachian Basin and pipe it to Pittsburgh, Cleveland, Akron, and other growing industrial cities of the region. By 1911, only two years after the formation of the Virginia Railway and Power Company, an integrated network of gas production, transmission, and distribution facilities had been assembled under the umbrella of Standard Oil Company. Already in place were four of the five companies that were to become the CNG system: The River Gas Company (founded in 1894); The Peoples Natural Gas Company (1885); Hope Natural Gas Company (1898); and The East Ohio Gas Company (1898). The final piece was added in 1930 when Standard organized a pipeline to supply non-affiliated utilities in New York State.

In the same way the "trust-busting" of the Public Utility Holding Company Act of 1935 changed business for the Virginia Railway and Power Company, in 1943 it also forced Standard to consolidate the five natural gas operations into a single, independent company — Consolidated Natural Gas Company.

TRANSMISSION AND DISTRIBUTION

In the post-World War II years, CNG's transmission and distribution operations grew rapidly, and the company made its first equity offering in 1947. Territorially, CNG extended its service area in Ohio from east of Cleveland to the Pennsylvania border with the purchase of Lake Shore Gas Company. It then became one of the first utilities to join the search for natural gas in the Gulf of Mexico, first as a partner in drilling ventures and, by 1962, as a

The Gulf of Mexico became a viable locale for natural gas production in the 1960s. CNG was one of the first utilities to enter the Gulf in 1957 and, by 1966, had established a full-scale exploration and production staff after several successes. Known for a proactive, progressive approach, CNG eventually became operator on many of its new leases, a move that served the company well in the 1970s when the prospects of gas shortages added a dimension of urgency to the search for new reserves. The company also began to seek out overlooked leases that experience showed to have good potential. By its 100-year anniversary in 1986, CNG had a strong presence in the Gulf, with several substantial discoveries.

STORAGE

Storage is vital to the natural gas business. It equalizes demand, absorbing excess gas during warm months and using it to meet winter demand peaks. In 1937, CNG began development of what eventually would become North America's largest natural gas storage capacity — 845 billion cubic feet — by converting depleted Appalachian gas fields into 26 underground storage pools. By 1988, storage had become another way to generate revenues through the sale of storage service to other pipelines and utilities.

A NEW NAME: DOMINION RESOURCES

CNG entered the electricity arena in the 1990s when it began buying and selling generation from wholesalers. "It was a way to help us maximize the value of our natural gas, but without our own substantial generation operations, we really couldn't compete," explained Davidson. The company explored joint ventures before entertaining thoughts of a merger. When the deal was finally struck, CNG no longer had to settle for a minor role on the industry stage. Instead, it became a key component in one of the 21st century's most formidable energy companies, Dominion Resources. ■

Just as VEPCO's Home Services department taught customers how to use electricity in their kitchens, CNG's Peoples Natural Gas Company taught customers how to use gas. Shown is a 1968 photo of a Home Services demonstration being recorded.

liquefied natural gas from Algeria; and a move into Canadian natural gas exploration. Through new nontraditional sales, it became the first company to tap the off-system market in a major way by selling natural gas and associated storage to neighboring pipelines and utilities. And in 1984, it expanded the wholesale market into New England, New Jersey, and metropolitan New York.

EXPLORATION AND PRODUCTION

By 1986, The Peoples Natural Gas Company's Well No. 1 in Murrysville, Pennsylvania, contributed only a trickle to CNG's gas production, but throughout the company's history, it has been a significant trickle. Drilled in 1886, the well marked the birth date of CNG's production. Over the subsequent four decades, wells drilled in the Appalachian Mountains and foothills were the nation's dominant source of natural gas.

Customers aren't just the folks who pay the bills — they're friends. Over the years, Dominion employees who have daily contact with the public — meter readers, linemen, and customer service reps — have forged lasting friendships with the people they serve. In this 1986 photo, meter reader Bobby Joe Dawson (*in truck*) caught up with Mr. Horn, a customer in Virginia's Allegheny District.

CHAPTER 4

Powering Relationships

EMPLOYEE RESOLVE, strong community service, and a philanthropic ethic don't get reported on the balance sheet. Nowhere on the income statement will you find a line item that captures corporate culture and values. But the people who work for Dominion represent a huge advantage for company owners and customers.

THOMAS F. FARRELL II

Chairman, President, and CEO

On a sultry New Orleans Saturday morning — August 27, 2005 — Deanka Green was finishing up her weekend chores when she flipped on the television and learned that Hurricane Katrina, a Category 3 storm that had already grazed Florida, was heading directly for the Crescent City, 80 percent of which is below sea level. "We're used to storms in the Gulf of Mexico," said Green, then an engineering analyst for Dominion's former Exploration & Production group. "We knew Katrina was coming our way, but we had no sense of urgency. It hit me Saturday — this is not like the others."

That Katrina was "not like the others" is an understatement. It wreaked havoc on the southeast, becoming one of the five deadliest hurricanes in American history and the country's largest humanitarian aid crisis since the Great Depression.

With production platforms dotting the Gulf, physical operations of its exploration and production offshore business headquartered in New Orleans, and 446 employees scattered throughout the area, Dominion experienced Katrina's impact firsthand. But even before the storm subsided, mobilization efforts began in Houston, Oklahoma City, and Richmond for a massive search to locate all affected Dominion employees. After each was found safe, Dominion became a safety net by assuring them

that their jobs, paychecks, and benefits would continue. Temporary housing was arranged, along with new office space — all within three weeks. "You had no time to stop and think about the magnitude of what we were taking on," said Donna Kelliher, director-Travel Services. "You just had to do it. Had we waited one more day to search for housing in Houston, we would have been at least two weeks behind in finding temporary housing and getting our employees back to work."

Meanwhile, 280 Dominion employees from Virginia and North Carolina drove to New Orleans

Dominion was the first out-of-state utility to reach the Gulf Coast and offer mutual aid when Hurricane Katrina hit in 2005. While Katrina did not directly affect Dominion's service area, it displaced 446 company employees based in New Orleans, Louisiana. Within a week, they were relocated and working in Houston, Texas.

to work alongside crews from other utility companies in the Herculean task of rebuilding the power grid. As the first utility offering mutual aid to reach the area, they worked in treacherous conditions. Some days they gave their lunches to hungry residents. At times they slept in their trucks. It was the largest mutual-aid deployment in company history. "No single utility can respond to a major catastrophic event like this," said Wade Briggs, a Dominion Virginia Power operations manager who was among the very first outside utility workers to arrive in hurricane-ravaged Jefferson Parish, Louisiana. "It requires a cooperative effort, and that is the essence of what we're about. We at Dominion know what it's like to be on the receiving end of help, so when a call comes in, we feel the need to respond."

Throughout the company, employees pitched in to raise $150,000 for the Dominion Katrina Relief fund, an amount matched by the company to help colleagues who suffered losses. Dominion also donated an additional $250,000 to the Salvation Army to assist with the larger community relief effort.

Dominion's timely and thorough response to the Hurricane Katrina catastrophe exemplifies how company employees react with purpose and confidence under pressure, just as they have in countless other crises that have affected the company in its 100-year history. But it also portrays a larger truth: that relationships — with employees, customers, unions, legislators, fellow utilities, shareholders, and communities — are critical to doing business the Dominion way.

"THIS ISN'T JUST A COMPANY, IT'S A FAMILY OF PEOPLE"

For all the changes Dominion has weathered over the past century, there has been one constant: Dominion could not do the essential, necessary work required to power the four million homes and businesses of today's customers without the knowledge, expertise, attention, and care of its 17,000 employees. "The company could not exist without its employees, and these same employees are equally dependent upon the company; one is indispensable to the other to carry on." S. R. Neesham made this statement in a 1927 employee newsletter; it could just as easily have been said in 2010.

For much of the 20th century, the company played a paternal role toward employees. Their trust was to be earned, not expected, and the company reciprocated with benefits and other job perks that reinforced the relationship. "The company must deserve and win the confidence, goodwill, and cooperation of all of its own employees … [or] it can never hope to have that necessary goodwill and friendship of the public, to win their confidence, if

These 22 managers oversaw the Employee Benefit Association in 1932. Early benefits included a per diem during disability and death benefits. Today, Dominion's benefits are broad, ranging from health, long-term care, and life insurance to tuition reimbursement and wellness incentives.

ALL IN THE FAMILY

Bradley C. "Cliff" Newman ... Bradley R. "Casey" Newman ... Robert "Bob" Newman ... Jason Newman. It may read like the roster of a family reunion, but the three generations of Newmans with Dominion ties are just one example of how employees are keeping it all in the family. Since the days of Virginia Railway and Power Company, employees have harbored a sense of pride for working at Dominion — so much so that they often recruit family members to apply for jobs.

Bradley C. "Cliff" Newman started in 1946 as a groundman; he retired in 1985 as superintendent of Construction. His older son, Bradley R. "Casey" Newman, a mechanic at Bellemeade Power Station in Richmond, came aboard in 1977. Robert "Bob" Newman, his younger son, now a lineman in Midlothian, started six years later in 1981. "While we were growing up, the company was very family-oriented; we were always going to picnics at the company, and I would end up looking at a board full of rope knots," remembered Bob Newman. "I was fascinated by that and wanted to do exactly what Dad was

Cliff Newman (*right*), sons Bob and Casey (*center left and right*), and grandson Jason (*left*) make working at Dominion a family affair. Cliff began his career in 1946. Jason started in 2008.

doing — be a lineman. But because Dad was a superintendent, he didn't think it would be a good idea for me to work under him. So I started as a mechanic and switched over later."

Jason Newman, Bob's son and Cliff's grandson, joined Dominion in 2008 as a project designer. "Every time the two of them were together that's all I heard — lineman talk," said the youngest Newman. "It was always '4KV this' or '477 that,' not to mention all their tales about transformers or potheads blowing up. After 24 years of hearing their stories at the dinner table, I figured I might as well come onboard just so I could understand their lingo." All jokes aside, his dad, uncle, and grandfather helped him realize that "it was a great company to work for and a great place to start my career."

The idea of hiring with a preference toward friends and family members of employees was widely accepted at the company for most of the 1900s. It made sense that good employees would naturally recommend like-minded friends and family members, and for the most part, this was the case. In the 1980s, however, policy changed. "We started having a few problems right before I became president, so I instituted a policy where we wouldn't hire children if the parent was still an employee," said Bill Berry, former chairman, president, and CEO, whose father, J. H. Berry, also worked for the company prior to his son joining VEPCO. "It cleared up the problem, but it created another problem: There were a lot of good kids who would have done a great job that we didn't hire. Later on, we ended up reversing it. A lot of employees were glad about that."

Joann Shriner, who retired in 1994 after 17 years with the company, is another legacy employee. She met her husband at work; they married a year later. "The same thing happened with my husband's parents," she said. "My father-in-law, Virmardel A. Shriner, was the manager of Northern Neck Power

Dixie Bryant celebrated fifty years with the company in 2008. "You won't find a better group of people than you have at Dominion," said Dixie. "This job has always been more than a paycheck." Her daughter, Dana, son, Owen, and daughter-in-law, Janice, also work for Dominion. *From left*: Janice Bryant, Dana Glass, Dixie Bryant, and Owen Bryant.

Station in Warsaw, Virginia. His wife, Elizabeth, was a secretary there. There were lots of husbands and wives who worked at the company back then."

Dominion's current hiring policy continues to welcome recommendations from employees for friends and family members. "Employees tend to refer people that value the same things that are important to Dominion," explained Demetrius Carter, supervisor-Staffing Strategy. "We are interested in finding those people who can truly embrace our culture and carry the company forward." Still, candidates are ultimately chosen based on their fit to the company. "Sometimes the best qualified person is not a good match for Dominion, and sometimes, a better-fitting candidate is chosen over someone with a referral. It's a good example of how we really focus on the core value of excellence."

In a 2006 employee engagement survey, 88 percent of employees said they would gladly refer a good friend or family member to Dominion for employment. No doubt it's for the same reasons that Robert Smith, a retired foreman and third-generation legacy employee, stayed for 40 years. "I think we've done well by the company and the company has stood by us," he said. "It's a good company, a big company, and a solid company — in economic times like these, that makes you feel pretty good." ■

The company's Volunteer Chorus was formed in 1986 and included 45 Richmond employees. Here the chorus performed at a 1987 holiday tree lighting ceremony on the steps of the Virginia State Capitol.

Throughout the company's history, employees have mixed work and play, as evidenced by this casual employee dinner in the 1960s.

Virginia Power executives and employees staffed the telephones for the Miracle Network Telethon in 1988.

Vice President Randy McIver's Southern District Management "team" at a teambuilding program for Commercial Operations managers. The team won gold "V" letterman jackets and a plaque for achieving their 1983 goals.

Departments and groups have always celebrated holidays, births, marriages, and career milestones together. Here, the Norfolk Sales department enjoyed their annual Christmas party sometime during the 1940s.

our own employees do not have such a feeling towards our company," said W. E. Wood, a former company president, in a 1928 *Vepcovian* article. "Nor will the public ever get along well with our employees if our employees do not get along well with each other. Good will is essential."

Goodwill in the form of benefits was the result of Virginia Railway and Power's 1911 merger with the Norfolk and Portsmouth Traction Company. Founded in 1903, the Norfolk division association offered members per diem benefits during disability; upon death, the member's beneficiary received $1 for each member in the association at the time of death. Richmond's first relief association eventually came along in 1915. It was one of the best in the industry; generally, only America's largest industrial organizations provided plans of this merit.

In 1927, the two groups merged to form the companywide Virginia Electric and Power Company Employee Benefit Association. It remained the primary source of benefits until 1945, when VEPCO implemented a retirement plan, group insurance, and hospitalization.

Taking its paternal role to heart, VEPCO continually offered new services to improve the well-being of its employees. In 1933, the company instituted the 40-hour work week, five years before the Fair Labor Standards Act made it law. Other personal services included distributing vitamin capsules to promote "the health and well-being of both men and women," providing free inoculations for typhoid fever, creating a circulating library so that employees "throughout the system may have the advantage of reading books which will be helpful to them in their work," and encouraging employees with an acre of land to implement a "Have More" plan to maximize its use and output.

In the 1920s, VEPCO began providing tuition reimbursement to employees, a practice that continues today. At the time, 200 workers participated in college courses, correspondence schools, night classes, and other studies designed to enhance employees' personal development so they would be prepared for "bigger service and higher places in the industry." Then, as now, the company believed that an "employee should take advantage of every opportunity to learn more about the business in which he is engaged and to supplement his store of knowledge with study and schooling which is now to be had so easily and in such a practical way."

The company even went so far as to offer advice in a 1954 *Vepcovian* newsletter to the wives of linemen:

Begin his day with a good breakfast and let him relax with coffee and his cigarette before leaving for work. Make a practice of telling him to be careful each morning. … When you're dressed to go out and the 'phone rings calling him to work, try not to act too disappointed; after all his job comes first. Try not to be too sympathetic concerning the bad weather in which he must work because if you are sympathetic, he begins feeling sorry for the old 'bread winner' and thinks of the weather even more. Then, "grin and bear it" when you're the only woman on the block who hangs out "Long Johns" on the clothesline and those creosote dungarees that never seem to come clean. Just remember those things are a part of your bread and butter.

AN OBLIGATION TO SERVE

The old-timers, or "lifers" as they were nicknamed because of spending their entire careers at the

THEN

Jeff Pitts, shown with his family, enrolled at the Richmond Professional Institute (now Virginia Commonwealth University) in 1952 under the company's Tuition Refund Program. Pitts earned his B.A. degree after 13 years of night classes. As early as 1931, 200 employees took advantage of the tuition refund program.

NOW

Kevin Dobbins (*left*), manager of Employee Services, joined Dominion (CNG) as a call center representative in 1995. As he earned promotions, he also pursued B.S. and M.S. degrees through the Tuition Reimbursement Program. Dominion spent almost $1.4 million in 2009 on educational assistance for employees.

company, were fiercely loyal to the company. "Good pay, good benefits, good job security — that's why I came to work at VEPCO," said Allan Greer Jones, maintenance coordinator at Bremo Power Station, who started with the company in 1972. "I think everybody is looking for that, and it's kind of hard to come by."

Chester Smith, who worked in engineering for "39-and-a-half good years," agreed. "The guy who offered me this job said you'll never become a millionaire but you'll always have a job if you work at a power company. … There's always work and there's always appreciation that you get for it."

Like Smith, Bradley C. "Cliff" Newman, who retired in 1985 after 39 years with the company, considered working at VEPCO a privilege. "I begged God to get me this

job, and I thought I owed the company something," he said. "I have my check stub still … $58 was the first pay I drew at VEPCO. They taught me a trade and they paid me generously. I was tickled to death to work here."

A steady job and paycheck weren't the only perks that convinced employees to stay. Working with electricity is dangerous; there is a bond created between people when they hold each others' lives in their hands.

A VEPCO employee handbook from the 1980s touted that employees were "carefully selected," and it is evident from the beginning that the company has recruited and attracted people who innately feel an obligation of service. Understanding the essential nature of the job, they have a work ethic that drives them to deliver — on time, without fanfare. "We're not a

Vepco
Employee Handbook
An Equal Opportunity Employer

company of people running around boasting about being the premier power company," said James "Jim" Norvelle, director-Media Relations. "Here, everybody has a job to do, they know what it is, and they just want you to get out of the way so they can do it."

A commitment to the job also meant a commitment to fellow employees who helped get it done. Bessie Lamkin, an employee in 1930, said that "whatever takes most of our time should mean most to us. It is in that sense, therefore, that I hold my title to membership in our business family as the greater part of my living."

Almost 80 years later, Randy McIver, a former vice president who retired in 1991 with 30 years' experience, spoke of his relationships in this way: "This wasn't just a company, it was a family of people. They gave a certain personality to the company … one of looking after each other and protecting each other … and I found that all the way through my career."

THE MODERN FACE OF DOMINION

Times have changed in the new millennium, and although Dominion no longer passes out vitamins or gives marital advice, the improvements in benefits, compensation, and training programs landed the company on *Business Week* magazine's 2008 list of "Best Places to Launch a Career."

"We try hard to do right by our employees," said Tom Farrell. "The type of work we're in attracts a certain type of person. If they want to be part of a company that's a vital part of the state's economic health and provides a public service, then this is the place to be." Although the family feeling remains, teamwork has become a better way to describe the company-employee relationship. All departments and companies, no matter how different, work

Mary C. Fray (*left*) of Culpeper, Va., was the first woman to serve on the company's Board of Directors in 1971 at a time when few women were welcome in corporate boardrooms. Fray was also the program chair for the Utility Women's Conference in 1985. Here, Fray posed with Ann H. Zinger, a director with American Electric Power and chair of the conference.

together as a team toward a shared goal. Moreover, the people most knowledgeable about a particular job are part of the decision-making process.

From a historical perspective, there have been great strides made in increasing the number of women and minorities in Dominion's workforce. Women, or "feminine additions," as they were called in the 1940s, are now represented at all levels in the company. In 1971, Mary Fray, a housewife and activist from Culpeper, Virginia, became the company's first female board member. "I was overcome — there were not very many women serving on boards anywhere," she said in a 1988 interview. "Often, I felt like Mrs. Vepco around this area because of the many times I was confronted with questions, [but] people need to be well-informed." Fray remained a vital part of the board for 16 years. "We were a traditional utility for so long, but I

really think the old mindset broke in the mid-1990s," said Pam Snider, director-Workforce Relations. "Dominion's overall attitude about women and minorities in the workforce has changed drastically since then."

African-Americans and people of other ethnicities, who were once prohibited from joining the Employee Benefit Association and limited to the most menial of jobs, now have open access throughout Dominion, including leadership and officer roles. Still, the efforts being made are considered as works-in-progress. "What is encouraging to me is that everybody is at the table to figure this out," said Teri Taylor, diversity consultant with Dominion. "We are not perfect and everyone knows that — including people at the senior levels of management, who aren't happy with that fact. And yet, as an African-American woman, I think we are definitely moving in the right direction."

With 45 percent of the company's workforce eligible for retirement in 2012, a big change is expected over the next few years in the physical makeup of the company's employees. Efforts also are being made to change the company mindset. "Our focus has moved away from the traditional way of doing things as a utility toward the idea that diversity — in backgrounds, leadership styles, and perspectives — makes Dominion a stronger company in the end," said Carol Zedaker, manager-Employee Relations and a 26-year Dominion employee.

Diversity initiatives such as employee councils and leadership diversity training reinforce Dominion's commitment to diversity in the workplace. In 2001, Dominion received the Large Company Diversity Award from the Richmond Human Resources Management Association for "leadership

Vickie Lewis and Dave Tabor, employees at Dominion East Ohio's 55th Street Center, added their personal touch to the Ohio Diversity Council mural as part of the festivities at the 2008 Diversity Day event. The mural depicts the Dominion East Ohio service area, with the Ohio Diversity Council logo as the center point.

ABOVE: The Northern Virginia Diversity Council hosted a "Heritage Day" festival in Warrenton, Virginia, in 2008. Employee Jerri Brooks (*front left*) performed an Irish step dance with her Irish folk dance troupe, the Aoibhneas an Rince Irish Dancers. LEFT: Dressed in a traditional Indian sari, employee Vishwa Bhargava demonstrated a variety of dance steps at the 2008 Diversity Day.

In 2009, Richmond employees participated in a Diversity Day celebration on Brown's Island, hosted by the Central Virginia Diversity Council. Organizing and participating in Diversity Days is one way the company recognizes and celebrates diversity throughout its workforce and the communities it serves.

Pam Simmons, a Dominion Transmission employee in Clarksburg, enjoyed the 2008 West Virginia Diversity Day events with Ben Hardesty, president-Dominion Exploration & Production.

ONE DOMINION

When Dominion merged with Consolidated Natural Gas in 2000, one of the components critical to success was the blending of two cultures and their myriad subcultures into one cohesive team. "Instead of building relationships externally, we had a new necessity of building relationships internally," explained Eva Teig Hardy, former executive vice president of Public Policy & Corporate Communications. "We had to make sure we came to consensus, and that we all understood that something in one area affects another." That shared vision of working together as a team evolved into one of the company's four core values: One Dominion.

Dominion employees are scattered across 18 states and the District of Columbia. They work in three different business units and a corporate services company. But they know the whole is greater than the sum of its parts. Together, they cross organizational boundaries to achieve a shared mission and purpose. It's teamwork at its best. It's "One Dominion."

And yet today's "One Dominion" is even more than teamwork — it's an attitude. Historically, Dominion's employees have always worked as a team, but unlike the days of the segregated South, the "One Dominion" of 2010 recognizes and celebrates the value and strength in the diversity of its work force.

A recent example of the teamwork and diversity of "One Dominion" in action is the establishment of the Dominion Memorial Scholarship Fund. In 2007, 32 people were killed in the shootings at Virginia Polytechnic Institute and State University in Blacksburg, three of whom were Dominion's own — students with a parent or grandparent who worked for the company. To honor the memory of the Virginia Tech students, the company annually awards six scholarships to exemplary college-bound high school seniors. The scholarships are renewable for up to three years.

In the spirit of "One Dominion," the program is open to all children and grandchildren of retired or current full-time Dominion employees. A special committee evaluates candidates on the basis of academic performance, community service, and leadership. During the first two years, 12 scholarships were awarded to students from Ohio, Pennsylvania, Texas, Virginia, and West Virginia who are attending universities throughout the country. The company is honored to help such outstanding teenagers begin and sustain their college careers. ■

In 1931, 227 employees of VEPCO's Mechanical department in Richmond posed in front of the Paint Shop on Robinson Street and Grayland Avenue. In 2009, half the property was occupied by the Greater Richmond Transit Authority; the other half housed a Dominion operations facility. J.T. Porter, superintendent of equipment in the 1930s, said that "much of our achievement has been due to the loyal and unfailing cooperation among the employees of this department as well as that of other employees in the other departments of our company."

in the Richmond business community in acknowledging, managing, and valuing diversity in the workplace." Then-CEO Tom Capps said at the time that "we can all feel good about that pat on the back acknowledging what we're doing right. But let's consider that pat on the back to be a push from behind to go even further." The Dominion of today is taking his advice to heart. "Anything that promotes tolerance and respect for individual differences — as diversity does — helps create the work environment we want at Dominion," said Farrell.

ONGOING LABOR RELATIONS

Throughout the company's history, there has been a lot of give-and-take between Dominion and the collective bargaining units representing its employ-

This 21st-century advertisement celebrates "The Power of Diversity" at Dominion. The company's philosophy is based on the belief that a work force and group of suppliers with different backgrounds and experience generates a broader range of ideas.

ees. At times, the relationship has been complicated, but more often than not, the parties have come to the table to work through important issues that matter to both sides. "Our relationship is much like a marriage," explained Jackson Wells, president of the International Brotherhood of Electrical Workers (IBEW) Local 50, which represents 3,365 members, or about 55 percent of Dominion's union-represented employees. "It's up and down. It can be contentious, but we have a method to resolve issues, and the company has been pretty

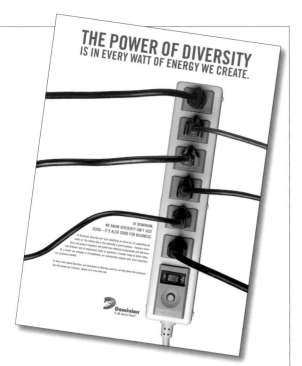

Dominion's stance on diversity has evolved dramatically over the past 100 years. Today, Dominion uses a broad definition of diversity to describe how individuals are both different and similar: "It includes age, physical ability, education, religion, ethnic background, socioeconomic status, economic region, personality, employment history, sexual orientation, position in the organization, race, gender, as well as other characteristics that make each of us unique individuals."

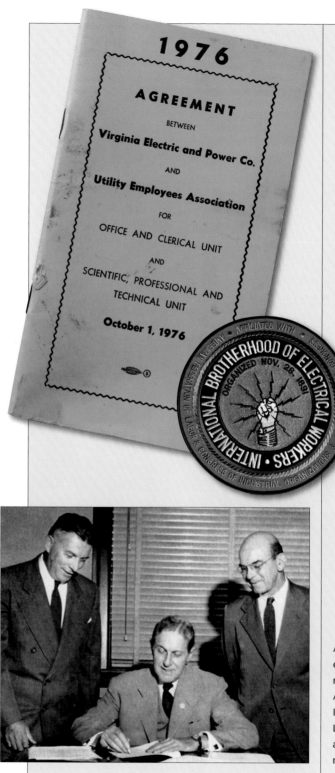

DOMINION'S CURRENT UNIONS

International Brotherhood of Electrical Workers
Local 15

International Brotherhood of Electrical Workers
Local 50

International Brotherhood of Electrical Workers
Local 326

International Brotherhood of Electrical Workers
Local 486

International Union of Operating Engineers
Local 310

United Steelworkers of America
Local 12502

Utility Workers Union of America
Local 69

Utility Workers Union of America
Local 308

Utility Workers Union of America
Local 310

Utility Workers Union of America
Local 464

Utility Workers Union of America
Local G555

A variety of unions have represented Dominion employees over the years. Today, 11 different bargaining units represent approximately one-third of employees. About 55 percent of all unionized employees are in International Brotherhood of Electrical Workers (IBEW) Local 50. Shown are a union agreement, IBEW patch, and lineman's belt buckle. *LEFT*: The signing of an agreement in 1956.

good with it so far. I might be head of the union, but hey, it's still my company, and I'm pretty proud to be an employee."

In 1937, the Independent Organization of Employees (IOE) became the first collective bargaining unit to represent company employees. Wages, safety, child labor, and long work days were among the concerns it addressed. The agreement between the union and the company provided other benefits such as free transportation on streetcars and buses, VEPCO contributions to the employee benefit association and group insurance plan, paid vacation, and educational courses.

Ten years later, in 1947, Virginia became a "Right to Work" state, ensuring the rights of people to work regardless of membership in any labor union. The unions, however, remained strong. In fact, Jack Holtzclaw, VEPCO's president in 1950, emphasized the company's good relations with its unions on the WRVA radio "Celebration Show":

Evil infiltration into the leadership of our labor unions has produced interruptions of vital services undertaken by our various public utilities. But in Virginia we have never had an interruption of these vital services. I hope the day will never come that we have such interruptions. I am satisfied that with wise counsel and leadership on both sides of the conference table, and with the benefits of the provisions of the Virginia Public Utilities Labor Relations Act, the public interest will always prevail.

In late 1979, as the company was slowly recovering from the turmoil of the 1970s, several salaried technical and professional employees pushed for the IBEW to replace the Utility Employees Association (UEA), which represented about 3,300 of

VEPCO's 10,500 employees at the time. With three parties involved, the election had the feel of a political campaign.

"When it came time to make a decision [about supporting one or the other], we sat around the conference room with a bunch of different people," former CEO Bill Berry remembered. "You got the sense that no one really wanted either union, but the chances of neither winning looked slim. When it got down to choosing one of the unions to support, I said I was willing to take the crapshoot."

Berry's gamble paid off. When the election was finally held in 1982, it was a 2-to-1 win for no union representation — an overwhelming defeat of the union proposal and an important vote of confidence for management. For the first time in 40 years, the company's salaried employees were union-free. At the time, it was the second-largest white collar union election in the history of the electric utility industry, and the largest such election in the preceding 42 years.

Only a few strikes have occurred in the company's electric history. One took place in 1964 over job descriptions, and another in 1978 when workers at Mt. Storm briefly staged a wildcat strike (a work stoppage not authorized by union officials). Most notable was a two-week strike in 2002, an action taken after union officials and management worked on a new contract for six months but couldn't agree on retirement and medical benefits.

Since then, the company has strived to keep the lines of communication open with the 12 different collective bargaining units that represent 37 percent of Dominion's employees. Today, safety continues to be a discussion topic, along with health care and retirement benefits. "We've had almost entirely positive relationships with our union representatives in the vast majority of cases," said CEO Farrell.

THE CUSTOMER: "A LIFELONG FRIEND"

In 1954, a customer walked into the Charlottesville, Virginia, office, announced that he had no electric power at home, and therefore had come to VEPCO to get some. Lionel Key, the local manager at the time, went along in good humor and told the customer to help himself. With that, the customer plugged in his electric razor and started shaving.

There are thousands of stories about Dominion employees doing the extra, the unexpected, or the unusual to make a customer happy — the trolley car operator who delivered packages to the door for elderly riders, the lineman who towed a customer's car from a ditch in the middle of a thunderstorm, the meter reader who repaired an oven's hinges because "they were about to fall off, and I wanted the customer to be safe." More recently, two East Ohio employees, Jeff Smith and Dave Mackey, rescued a five-year-old boy from a tragic accident. The two happened upon the wreck just after it occurred; their quick thinking and handy tools helped them free the boy from underneath the SUV just as hot antifreeze and diesel fuel began leaking into the vehicle. "If we had come through 30 seconds earlier, we might not have seen the accident," said Mackey. "Or if we had come through 30 seconds later, we would have been caught up in a traffic jam and might not have been able to help in time."

A century of good deeds and good service stand behind Dominion's reputation as a good neighbor. It's a role that evolved in part because of the mystery of electricity. "I've talked to people who thought that electricity was something in between two walls of the room that, when you plugged in an appliance,

Quick action by Dave Mackey (*left*) and Jeff Smith (*right*), Dominion East Ohio employees, saved a five-year-old boy from entrapment under a wrecked SUV. In their spare time, Smith and Mackey volunteer on coal mine rescue teams in Kentucky.

would just be sucked out," said former CEO Berry.

That mystery, combined with the dependency of modern life on electricity to perform the simplest of functions, demands that Dominion fully lives up to its role as a public servant. "We are a public utility, and the word 'public' is very important," explained Norvelle. "In a sense, it's a parental relationship. Customers view us as guardians; they're not always happy about us playing that role, but they do expect that — and there's a trust in our relationship because of that."

The definition of "customer service" has evolved over time. In VEPCO's early days, the emphasis was clearly on growth and distribution. Once customers were "hooked up to power," any further service provided was reactionary: solving problems, responding to outages, explaining bills. Still, VEPCO recognized that many of these issues could be resolved easier and more quickly if the customer was greeted personally and pleasantly by a company employee. "[If] our personal representatives can be made efficient, intelligent, and courteous enough,

STORM CHASERS

An early winter storm swept through New Jersey in November 1951, leaving a trail of destruction throughout the northeast part of the state. Trees crashed down, carrying with them distribution and transmission lines; some poles snapped like twigs, while others listed with the heavy gale. By the time the winds, sleet, and snow had ceased, 70,000 of Jersey Central Power and Light Company's 80,000 customers were without electric service.

Within 24 hours, crews from VEPCO were already on their way to help. They worked in freezing rain — the storm was still raging when they arrived — and mountainous sections covered in knee-deep snow. Most of the digging was done in frozen ground and broken rock, and stabilizing trees with guy wires was standard practice. Working day and night with little time for sleeping and eating, the crews finally returned home 12 days after being beckoned by the storm.

That scenario has been repeated countless times since, because the ability to create and deliver electricity hinges on an unpredictable and unavoidable factor: the weather. When Mother Nature doesn't cooperate, utilities rely on their relationships with fellow utilities to get the power on as soon as possible. Known as *mutual aid*, this reciprocal relationship is unique to the utility industry. It's the golden rule in action. "We are at our best during these events," said Keith Wooldridge, retired vice president-Energy Conservation and Customer Solutions. "You don't see a lot of mistakes; you see a lot of focus."

Dominion's first participation in mutual aid projects is unknown, but given that an obligation to serve the public is a like-minded mission for all utilities, it is probably a practice as old as the company itself. Formal mutual aid most likely began sometime after 1933, when VEPCO joined the Southeastern Electric Exchange as a founding member. VEPCO participated in the 1950s creation of the first storm planning/mutual aid committee, and was later active in developing the first mutual aid assistance guidelines for the group.

The earliest record of VEPCO answering the call for help is 1938, when eight employees were dispatched to Providence, Rhode Island, to help the Blackstone Valley Gas and Electric Company restore power after a hurricane and tidal waves pounded the coast from Long Island Sound to Vermont. Blackstone Valley's president, David Daly, praised the men for their conduct and efficiency, noting that:

I was immediately impressed by their fine appearance as they looked like a football squad starting out to win. We heard nothing but high praise of their training and ability as linemen, and our operating forces were particularly impressed by the ease in which they tackled our distribution system and dovetailed into our line organization.

Predictions of tropical storms and hurricanes trigger evacuations for most of the population. Not so for Dominion employees, who are ready to serve. Ray Golding Jr., a lineman from Virginia Beach, Virginia, is a veteran of hurricanes, as evidenced by his truck tally. When a catastrophe occurs, crews often work hundreds of miles away from their homes.

VEPCO line crews and their special airplane provided mutual aid to Rhode Island after a 1938 hurricane. The crew could cover 600 miles of ground in two-and-a-half hours by air. "Not one man lost one single day due to his inability to make it, and the men never forgot they were gentlemen," touted a story in a 1938 *Vepcovian*.

In March 1962, Richmond was hit with its worst snowstorm in 20 years. Seventy crews from outlying locations in Virginia and North Carolina, as well as independent crews from Richmond and Lynchburg, worked around the clock to restore service in four days. A few days later, a rain and windstorm hit the coast with 80-mile-per-hour winds and some of the highest tides in the area's history. The damage was so severe that President John F. Kennedy declared it a disaster area.

John Thurston, who retired in 1986 as central division supervisor of construction after 40 years with the company, remembered working on a crew sent to help out with a particularly harsh snowstorm in Maryland. "The people were just devastated," he said. "They were burning up the porch furniture and burning up the railings just to keep warm … because they didn't have electricity. If they could, any way at all, they'd come out and bring cookies and clap and carry on when they saw you coming in. They were glad to see us."

Just as Dominion has sent crews throughout the United States, the company also has been on the receiving end of such aid. While Hurricane Katrina indirectly affected Dominion's employees in the southeastern part of the United States, it was Hurricane Isabel in 2003 that caused the most damage to date to the company's electric service area. Concentrated in Dominion's service area, Isabel toppled hundreds of thousands — if not millions — of trees. Drenching rains flooded hundreds of homes and businesses. More than 1.8 million of Dominion's 2.2 million electric distribution customers were without power — a whopping 81 percent.

Eighteen utilities came to Dominion's aid from two mutual-aid agreement groups — Edison Electric Institute and the Southeastern Electric Exchange — that supply workers to help in a major outage. In the end, Dominion deployed 3,000 contractors and 3,500 mutual-aid workers to rebuild the infrastructure of a 30,000-square-mile service area, almost from the ground up. At the peak of the restoration, 12,000 workers were on the job, and in all, 63,000 hotel rooms were booked. A thousand truckloads brought materials from as far away as Colorado, with Dominion using 10,705 poles, 14,610 crossarms, 1,000 miles of wire, and 7,900 transformers — a supply that would have normally lasted from one to two years. "To have gone through a million man-hours of work, under extreme pressure and in the media spotlight, and to not have a serious accident or fatality, is a tribute to Dominion," said Wooldridge.

After the first week, the company met its goal of restoring service to more than 75 percent of the customers affected. In all, it took around-the-clock manpower for two weeks, with many workers putting in 14- to 16-hour days. "It's not one company in these storms; it's not one person — it's everybody helping everybody," said Ed Bushee, who retired as Safety department superintendent in 1985 after 36 years with the company. "In Katrina, we had crews all the way from Canada and the far side of the Midwest. When Isabel hit our own system, crews showed up from as far away as Oklahoma Gas & Electric, Hydro-Québec, and Florida Power & Light. The same people that you worked for, in turn, show up and are here working for you. Everybody does their share." ■

No one appreciates a utility worker more than a customer who has been without power for an extended length of time. Signs, homemade cookies, hot chocolate, sandwiches, handshakes, and hugs are a few of the ways customers say "thank you."

On April 26, 1937, waters of the Rappahannock River reached the highest stage ever recorded, cresting at 38.21 feet above the mean sea level at Embrey Power Station in Fredericksburg, Virginia. The surging waters carried away almost everything in their path, including three sections of the Free Bridge connecting Fredericksburg with Stafford and King George Counties. Thanks to quick-thinking workers who kept the station functioning, service was interrupted for only five hours.

On August 29, 1950, VEPCO connected its 500,000th customer, Mr. and Mrs. Adrian Murray of Halifax County, Virginia. The average cost of electricity per kilowatt hour was 2.78 cents; the average annual use was 2,004 hours.

In 1998, Scott and Paula Euerle of Virginia Beach, Virginia, pictured with meter reader Ben Nelson, became Dominion's two millionth customer. The average cost of electricity per kilowatt hour was 8.1 cents; the average annual use was 12,975 hours. "Who 50 years ago would have dreamed that they would be able to bake a potato in a microwave in just a few minutes?" asked Virginia Power President Norman Askew at the ceremony. "Who would have imagined ... that they could reach relatives and friends across the world via computers and the Internet?"

VEPCO's 750,000th customer was connected in 1960. The home of Mr. and Mrs. E. L. Wilder of Alexandria, Virginia, featured "150 ampere service and complete housepower wiring." The average cost of electricity per kilowatt hour was 2.46 cents; the average annual use was 3,984 hours.

Mr. and Mrs. Ray F. Rollins of Chesapeake, Virginia, were connected in 1971 as the company's one millionth customer. The average cost of electricity per kilowatt hour was 2.08 cents; the average annual use was 8,957 hours. The couple is shown with Harrison Hubard, VEPCO's eastern division vice president.

our patrons' unfavorable reaction to the use of our service can be largely ameliorated by the fascination of a pleasing human contact," claimed a 1928 *Vepcovian* article.

As more customers were connected and the cost of electricity increased, the company's role shifted to one of maintenance and reliability. Later, when electric rates spiked upward, customers also became concerned with efficiency and conservation. "Our customers have been educated to expect continuous satisfactory service from their electric servant, *Reddy Kilowatt*," said J. H. Berry, superintendent of the Electric department of the Norfolk Division in 1943 and the father of Bill Berry, who became the company's chairman, president, and CEO. "His name is *Reddy* and when a customer snaps on a switch she expects him to jump. He has done this all these years so consistently that any failure now is a keen disappointment."

W.O.W.-ING THE CUSTOMER

Being reactive to customer service issues solved the problem at hand but, over time, the company grew much more interested in being proactive. It was a lesson learned the hard way. In the 1970s, the company had difficulty communicating with its customers. "I think at the time that VEPCO didn't know which way to communicate because of the trepidation over energy shortages and embargoes," said Sylvia M. Solhaug, who chaired the company's customer consulting group in 1984. "VEPCO was not sure about what to communicate to its customers and was not as clear about the future. The company was a little short on giving people information and that made people feel disconcerted."

Moving forward, the challenge became one of identifying future issues and addressing them *before* they mushroomed into full-blown problems. With this logic in mind, the company began investing considerable time, talents, and money on surveys and opinion polls, beginning in 1981, to find out what customers want from their utility. "The difference is that before, we provided customers with what we thought they wanted," explained Becky Merritt, director of Customer Service Centers and a 31-year employee. "Today, we are more interested in asking them what *they* want. And we not only have to be willing to hear what they say, but we need to respond one way or another."

The definition of excellent customer service varies from one day to the next, and it's not something that only one department delivers. Rather, there is an emphasis on providing each customer with the *W.O.W. factor*, providing *What's needed, On time,* and *With value.* For example, the Call Center might receive calls from customers speaking up to 17 different languages in any given month. To decrease the duration of the phone call, the company implemented a translation service available around-the-clock for non-English speaking customers. "We want to provide elite end-to-end service, which means we have to coordinate our problem-solving with other departments in the company," said Merritt. "But it's a race, a continual process, because as fast as our society moves, what we are delivering today to satisfy the customer can be totally different from what will satisfy them tomorrow."

Technology has revolutionized customer service. With 2.4 million residences and businesses to serve electrically, the days of one-on-one contact with each customer for each issue are over. Still, Domin-

THEN

As recorded in *The Vepcovian* in April 1943: "All outside lines are busy! And so were all the lines coming in during the sleet storm, when operators ate their meals at the switchboard and some slept at the Exchange during the night so as to be on the job late and early." Shown (*left to right*) were Misses Hopkins, Berry, and Mariner, operators on the Richmond switchboard.

NOW

In 2009, customer service focuses on "first call resolution." Rather than taking as many calls as possible during their shifts, representatives try to resolve each issue on the first call. Individual calls may run longer than expected, but customers are spared the inconvenience of multiple calls. Shown is Shawnda Toler, a training assessment and performance coach in Richmond.

ion has implemented several options that provide customers with direct, immediate service. In 2009, more than two million transactions occurred via the Internet; most dealt with billing and payments, service requests, and outage reports. The telephone continues to be the medium of choice for customers, and with several self-serve options, 30 percent of the seven million calls received annually are addressed immediately by automated means. Mail, fax, and e-mail are additional ways customers can communicate with the company.

Because so many issues have the potential to hamper customer relations, Dominion is ever mindful that keeping customers happy is key to the company's success. "We look out for customers like

a lifelong friend," claims the 2008 Annual Report. "Dependable service is a given. Helpful programs to manage energy use and costs are at the ready, as are smiling faces or friendly voices on the phone."

SHAREHOLDERS: "DOMINION'S ULTIMATE OWNERS"

Maintaining relationships with existing investors, cultivating new investors, "talking up" Dominion at public functions and industry conferences, hosting investor meetings and earnings calls — it's all part of the job for Dominion's Investor Relations (IR) team.

Investors, both individuals and institutions, have long been an important part of Dominion. Nurturing the relationship in a formal manner,

REDDY KILOWATT

Reddy Kilowatt was conceived in 1926 after his creator, Ashton B. Collins, general commercial manager of the Alabama Power Company, came home from an industry convention pondering the idea of how to convince customers that electricity was indeed a "servant of mankind." Looking out the window into a thunderstorm, Collins witnessed a lightning strike and "at that moment Reddy Kilowatt sprang from his brow full-grown, like Athena from that of Zeus." In no time, Reddy became the mascot for more than 300 investor-owned utilities around the country, with coloring books, night lights, cigarette lighters, coffee mugs, thermometers, patches, pencils, and lapel buttons among the memorabilia created. In 1998, the Northern States Power Company (now part of Xcel Energy) acquired the image, which is currently managed by The Reddy Kilowatt Corporation. ∎

ABOVE LEFT: A Reddy Kilowatt tie clasp. *LEFT*: A 1945 Reddy Kilowatt poster from World War II urging customers to write to servicemen overseas. *RIGHT*: A Reddy Kilowatt mascot figurine.

Modern marketers consider Reddy Kilowatt to be one of America's top 20 product mascots. Shown is a night-light, one of many types of customer giveaways.

I'm a busy little atom I split myself in two,
I multiply as many times as I have jobs to do.
In summer, winter, spring or fall
I'm ready every hour;
Just push a switch and watch me zip
With . . . light . . . or heat . . . or power.

Reddy Kilowatt
YOUR ELECTRIC SERVANT

ABOVE: This Reddy Kilowatt poem appeared on another promotional item — a charm — to be placed on a bracelet or key ring. *BELOW*: Reddy promoted patriotism in his 1956 "Don't Forget to Vote" cartoon.

DON'T FORGET TO **VOTE**

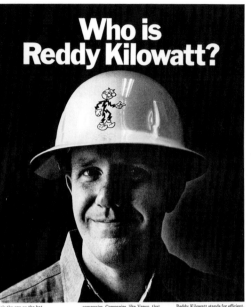

Who is Reddy Kilowatt?

He's the one on the hat.
You've seen his friendly face many times: on Vepco trucks, in ads like this, and on your electric bill.
But do you know what he stands for?
Reddy Kilowatt is a symbol of investor-owned, tax-paying electric utility companies. Companies, like Vepco, that are dedicated to furnishing you better electric service at lower cost.
Thanks to the skill of Vepco employees, and the most modern facilities and techniques, electricity is one thing that costs *less* now than it used to.

Reddy Kilowatt stands for efficient, dependable, low cost electricity. But the guy under the hat makes it possible.

Vepco a powerful lot . . . for powerful little

As late as the 1970s, VEPCO used Reddy Kilowatt in advertising campaigns.

Educational cartoons appeared weekly in thousands of newspapers and utility publications throughout the country. This one ran in *The Vepcovian* in 1945.

TOP: VEPCO chief lobbyist Bill Crump was nicknamed "Reddy Kilowatt" early in his career by Virginia legislator Joe Blackburn. In a caricature drawn personally for Crump, Pulitzer Prize-winning cartoonist Jeff MacNelly of the *Richmond News Leader* captured the lobbyist's reputation among Virginia legislators. *ABOVE*: Virginia Governor Mark Warner (*left*) talking with Crump in 2003 about state politics.

VEPCO President Pete McDowell presided over the company's 53rd annual meeting of shareholders in 1963. Said McDowell, "Of the 30 electric utility companies with revenues of $100 million or more in 1961, we rank 14th in revenues and 10th in net income." He also noted that VEPCO was "engaged in a gigantic construction program which will almost double present generating capacity by 1966." Projects included the 200,000-kilowatt Gaston Hydroelectric Station at Roanoke Rapids, North Carolina, and three in Virginia: a 220,000-kilowatt addition to the Possum Point Station, a similar-sized unit at Portsmouth Station, and 330,000 kilowatts of steam generation at Chesterfield Power Station.

however, was born of the tumultuous 1970s. In 1981, realizing the need to strengthen relationships with professional financial analysts, the company formed the Investor Relations department. Their early initiatives laid the foundation for Dominion's successful program today.

Stakeholders are financially tied to the company's vision: Dominion's success is their success. "They are the ultimate owners of the company; we are caretakers of their capital," explained Thomas E. Hamlin, a former analyst who studied Dominion and is now vice president-Financial Analysis & Investor Relations for the company. "Our job is to take care of them the best way we can — by investing their money in the business so that it produces good returns."

Part of the job involves keeping shareholders abreast of the company's current operations and vision for the future. "IR bridges the gap between company-speak and street-speak to make sure both sides understand each other," explained Joe O'Hare, vice president-Budgeting, Business Planning & Market Analysis.

The relationship is reinforced with honesty and candor. "They [IR] are the voice of the company to investors," said Po Cheng, an analyst with Longbow Capital who has been covering Dominion for 10 years. "Dominion's IR is one of the better groups — more open and transparent about giving information. Indirectly, if they were not so accessible, analysts might view management as closed and [it would] make them wonder why."

In the old days, utility stocks like VEPCO were favored by investors looking to balance their stock portfolios with a stable, safe investment. These stocks, often called "widows-and-orphans stocks,"

were considered low-risk and a sure bet for reliable income even in times of economic downturns. After all, everybody needs electricity.

In the 1980s, as competition began to creep into the utility business, that perception changed. As Dominion diversified into new markets with acquisitions of oil and gas reserves, international power plants, telecom businesses, and real estate, the stock began to look less like that of a traditional utility stock. "In other words, we have not been getting top dollar for the fruits of our labor because we were selling apples and oranges in the same bag," said Farrell. "Those who wanted only the apples (reliable, safe earnings from the wires, pipes, storage, and generation businesses) did not want to purchase the oranges (high growth, more volatile earnings from the E&P business), and vice versa."

Although many of the diverse businesses Dominion ventured into were profitable, ultimately the decision to sell many of the ventures, including the Exploration & Production business, proved sound. "I've studied the company since the 1980s, and Dominion has a history of being innovative," said Hamlin. "The company wasn't afraid to try new things but it also wasn't afraid to go back to the basics when it made sense."

THE CUSTOMER STOCK PURCHASE PLAN

One of the company's most creative ideas was conceived as a way to better serve individual shareholders. In 2009, buying stock directly from a company is commonplace, but in 1980, it was a revolutionary idea — and it was VEPCO's. If the company learned anything from the tumultuous 1970s, it was that the more customers understand the power business, the more empathetic they are to VEPCO when outside factors — oil shortages, inflation, fuel costs — affect the company. According to Linwood R. Robertson, the former executive vice president and chief financial officer who oversaw the process, creating a stock purchase plan was a triple win: "It was good for our shareholders, our customers, and for the company."

VEPCO ironed out the operational logistics while awaiting approval from the U.S. Securities Exchange Commission. The launch came in 1980 and quickly gained attention as America's first customer stock purchase plan. Participants received coupon booklets and made monthly payments into the plan for as little as $10. At the end of the 12-month period, the payments, plus interest paid by VEPCO, were used to buy common stock directly from the company without incurring brokerage fees or commissions. Any dividends were automatically reinvested. "It was part of our evolution of reaching out to our customers and encouraging them to have not only an interest — but an invested interest in the company," observed Patty Wilkerson, retired vice president and corporate secretary.

In September 1981, VEPCO issued 544,163 shares of common stock valued at more than $6 million. By year-end, 14,000 customers had subscribed to VEPCO shares under the plan; half had never before purchased a share of common stock in any company. In 1996 the plan became Dominion Direct, an open enrollment, direct stock purchase program. Investors no longer use monthly coupons; instead they can contribute money whenever they want and the company purchases shares twice a month.

Lindy Hill, a retired educator from Highland Springs, Virginia, and his wife, June, began investing monthly in the plan in 1992. "People will always need energy," said Hill. "Dominion is diversified in several different types of energy, they are well-managed, and they're local. I know people who have worked there for years, and that tells you a whole lot about the company."

Within a few years of approving this ground-breaking plan, the SEC changed its rules regarding individual investing. The stock plan also helped restore the company's public image, which had

TOP: Samples of VEPCO and Dominion stock certificates, as well as the 1982 Customer Stock Purchase Plan bill insert that invited customers to take part. It stated that "over 20,000 VEPCO customers subscribed to the plan last year." LEFT: With the exception of 1919 to 1924, Dominion has paid common stock dividends at least annually (in most years more frequently) since 1911.

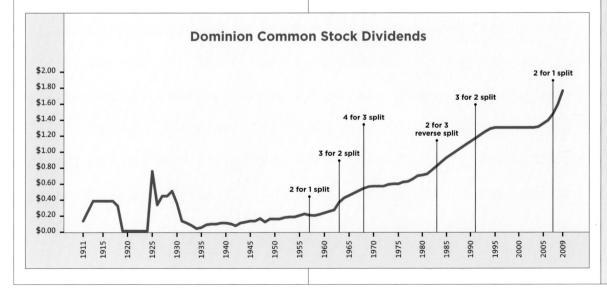

Dominion Common Stock Dividends

been battered throughout the 1970s. "It was very creative and an example that we were doing things differently from the old VEPCO," said Wilkerson. The program initially created a lot of very small accounts, which can be expensive administratively, but the company wanted the plan to be accessible to all customers. As Robertson summarized: "People saw that it was surprisingly easy to invest directly, and they stuck with it."

POWERING VIRGINIA

In 1929, *For the Old Dominion* made its "picturized" debut at theaters across the Commonwealth. Touted as "Two Thousand Feet of Interesting and Entertaining Pictures," the 30-minute film, sponsored by VEPCO, was designed to show that "Tidewater Virginia is not only replete with historical interest, but that it is also a live center of manufacturing enterprises driven by electric power supplied by the VEPCO system."

Considering the novelty of both electricity and motion pictures in the 1920s, *For the Old Dominion* was a major publicity coup for Virginia's growing electric company. The Commonwealth's first major economic upswing was under way, and VEPCO did its part by electrifying homes in cities and rural areas as fast as its service department could meet the demand. The film was a clever campaign to promote electricity usage, but it also acknowledged publicly the integral relationship between VEPCO and the Commonwealth: The growth of one was dependent upon the growth of the other.

Following the Great Depression, VEPCO formally created an Industrial Development department in 1936 to coordinate economic development initiatives throughout the company's service area. Then-president Jack Holtzclaw commented that:

With the considerable expansion which has taken place throughout the Virginia Electric and Power Company system during the past several years … Virginia and the adjacent areas are now in a position, as never before, to encourage industrial development particularly in rural and suburban areas, and to present their advantages to both new and existing industries who wish to expand or decentralize their present operations. … Our company is desirous of cooperating in every way we can with the various planning commissions, chambers of commerce, railroads, and other groups now studying and planning further industrial and economic development within the extensive area served by the VEPCO power system.

When World War II began, Virginia entered its second economic upturn. The war effort required additional power to manufacture supplies at Virginia-based factories, but also to power major military bases established in Virginia. VEPCO, along with government analysts, had predicted usage would decline after the war, but the boom continued. Veterans and their families wanted homes and businesses fully powered by electricity.

VEPCO also went to work attracting industries to its service area that could use its extra energy capacity. "Ad campaigns promoted VEPCO Country, the 'Top of the South,' to industries throughout the northeast," remembered William Stafford, who retired as Dominion's director of Economic Development in 2000. "We realized we were only as strong as the economies of the communities we were privileged to serve. Making business and industry strong resulted in more meters turning faster."

Additionally, VEPCO had encouraged companies throughout the war to expand facilities to make room for displaced farm workers. Together, these relationships evolved into an Area Development department focused solely on encouraging economic development.

As noted in *The Vepcovian* in May 1963, "J. R. Perrow (standing), manager of VEPCO's Area Development department, reviews an economic study with members of his staff. The department recently prepared and presented its 108th study."

Industry survey books and community profiles were prepared at no cost. Prospecting trips were conducted throughout the United States to attract industry. Advertisements were even published in *The Wall Street Journal*, *Fortune*, and other trade magazines promoting the advantages of doing business in Virginia. So successful were VEPCO's efforts that Virginia created a Division of Industrial Development in the early 1950s patterned after VEPCO's Area Development department.

RE-ENERGIZING RELATIONSHIPS

VEPCO's economic development was almost non-existent in the 1970s. The Middle East oil embargo and other crises had demanded the company's attention for most of the decade. When the 1980s commenced, the turmoil began to settle and VEPCO was able to finally turn its attention back to relationships, including those with business leaders and state and local officials.

In 1981, the Economic Development and Energy Services department was organized. Virginia was becoming a hot prospect for companies seeking stable tax rates, a clean environment, and a healthy business climate. Emphasis also had shifted away from manufacturing. "We are going after brainpower instead of horsepower," said Scott Eubanks, then director of the Virginia Division of Industrial Development. "By this, I mean companies that rely on state-of-the-art ideas and equipment. They are typically information- and communication-oriented and include research activities as well as assembly plants."

Courting technology companies continued in the 1990s, with former Governor George Allen coining the term "Silicon Dominion" to reflect the state's vibrant economic status. Allen also acknowledged that Virginia Power's competitive electric rates helped attract heavy hitters of high-tech to the state. But that wasn't all. With interests in Latin America, South America, the United Kingdom, and Europe, Dominion found itself encouraging economic development in other parts of the world. "I can't say enough about what Dominion has done for the Commonwealth of Virginia, but if you look at the big picture, they have played an important role in helping the economy of many different countries grow," said Benjamin J. Lambert III, a director of the company since 1994.

Today, Dominion no longer has business interests in other countries, but it continues to develop and sustain relationships with Virginia's long-time companies, new businesses attracted to the state, and government officials who promote economic development. "We have excellent relationships and a record of success in terms of working with governors and members of the General Assembly," said Eva Teig Hardy, retired executive vice president of Public Policy & Corporate Communications. Tom Farrell agrees. "We went through a period of deregulation in Virginia for about ten years. We've gone into re-regulation in Virginia. But over all these years, we've worked as hard as we can to have a good relationship with the regulators and the political infrastructure of the state, because it's important for them and important for us."

While the types of companies it tries to attract has changed, the Economic Development department is charged with the same task as it was almost 100 years ago: stimulating growth in Dominion's electric service areas in Virginia and North Carolina.

The history of Dominion is intertwined with the history of Virginia. In 1990, Eva Teig Hardy, former executive vice president of Public Policy & Corporate Communications, and Tom Capps, former Dominion chairman, president, and CEO, congratulated Douglas Wilder (*center*) on his election as Virginia's 66th governor.

Low operating costs and readily available electric and telecom infrastructure have contributed to the state's ability to woo 36 data centers to Northern Virginia alone. With each data farm using as much electricity as 6,000 homes, Dominion must be prepared to generate an amount of electricity comparable to the demand of a mid-sized city. "Virginia's economic boom is the product of a winning combination," said Farrell. "Our economic development community and elected leaders deserve tremendous credit. Sound fiscal and tax policies have always been a hallmark of Virginia state government. No wonder *Forbes* recognizes Virginia as the best state in the nation in which to do business." ◆

When Betty Belanger, Midlothian meter reader, approached Clara Howlett's South Richmond home one day in 1986, she didn't get her usual cheerful greeting. Instead, after knocking and listening, she heard a faint response from inside. Belanger opened the door and found Howlett on the floor, unable to stand after suffering a fall the prior day. Having participated in Virginia Power's Gatekeeper Program that focused on the safety of elderly customers, Belanger had been trained to immediately call rescuers and the Area Agency on Aging. "I knew the numbers and just what to do," she said. Fortunately, Howlett's condition was not serious, and she visited with Belanger on her porch shortly thereafter.

CHAPTER 5

The Heart of Dominion

**AS I HAVE GROWN OLDER,
it becomes clearer and clearer
that the things that really matter
are not what we obtain for
ourselves, but what we do for
the sake of others.**

ROBERT D. HAGY

Director-Gas Operations
Dominion East Ohio
and 2007 Dominion Volunteer of the Year

Every fourth Thursday of the month, Lola S. Ausby, joint utility administrator in Roanoke Rapids, North Carolina, hops into her car to make the lunchtime rounds for the local Meals on Wheels program. After work, she heads out for an evening of meetings: She's in her 25th year as elected town commissioner for Garysburg, North Carolina, where she is also the town's mayor pro tem and finance and budget officer. She has been the secretary and treasurer for the Ladies Auxiliary for the past 30 years. At Roanoke Salem Baptist Church, she holds down multiple positions: chair of Christian education, a deaconess, director of Vacation Bible School, member of the Women of Vision choir, and the instructor for the new members class. Oh, and it's only worth mentioning that her day could well have started with a wakeup alert from her scanner — she's the secretary and longtime member of the Garysburg Volunteer Fire Department.

It is a typical day of service for Ausby, a two-time winner of Dominion's Volunteer of the Year award, in 1994 and 2000, and the 2008 recipient of the Governor of North Carolina's Award for Outstanding Volunteer Service. "I guess it was something I was born with," she said. "I always knew, even in college, that I wanted to come back to Garysburg and give back to my community."

Throughout the Dominion network, there are lots of "Lolas," employees with a willingness and heart to serve without pay or publicity. "I think that employees see how blessed they are," explained Ausby. "I mean, you look at people who don't have what you have and you want to help someone. The need is there, and nothing is too small. It's the little things a lot of times that mean the most."

"The gifts of time, money, and skill are important aspects of the volunteer experience, which is incredibly diverse and multifaceted," said Tom Farrell, chairman, president, and CEO. "But stripped of its many layers and outward differences, volunteering

Dominion employee and volunteer Lola Ausby sometimes has three meetings to attend in one night for different charitable organizations. "It's hard to choose which one to attend," she says. "I enjoy helping people — I've got this desire to make things happen, and I think that people like me can also encourage other people to do things."

"BE GLAD THAT YOU ARE ABLE TO GIVE"

In the 1930s, company employees gave generously to Richmond's Community Fund to underwrite a variety of community programs to help the indigent and needy. Today, Dominion remains a top supporter of the Fund, now known as the United Way. The following appeal from the November 1930 issue of The Vepcovian *illustrates that the more things change, the more they indeed stay the same.*

Fire risk is destructive to economic prosperity in any community. Lack of safety devices in large industries greatly increases expenditures for accidents. We build bridges so we won't fall into rivers and ravines; we place railings along mountain roadways: we do all sorts of things to prevent catastrophes in everyday life.

We know that destitution, disease and crime impair development, lessen civic pride and add to the burdens of taxation. Yet we are more or less indifferent to the prevention of these. We are willing to cure them, but we are often not willing to think ahead and ward them off.

VEPCO president Jack Holtzclaw (*third from right*) and Richmond mayor J. Fulmer Bright visited a city orphanage during the 1931 Community Fund drive.

The 39 agencies of the Community Fund are working together for the welfare of Richmond. Eight of them care for dependent children, four give their time to the relief and rehabilitation of families, six care for the sick and promote health, five protect the helpless, five give general civic and social education, and 11 build health and character for the young people of our city.

When you are asked for your 1930-31 Community Fund pledge, remember that it is far better to keep boys and girls from falling than it is to pick them up after they have fallen.

During the Great Depression, these African-American employees at Richmond's 12th Street Power Station averaged $14 per 40-hour week in pay. Still, they managed to donate $5 each (equal to $80 today) to propel the plant to "Blue Ribbon" status in the 1934 Community Fund Campaign. The Community Fund was a precursor to the United Way.

begins with caring. It is the spark that ignites the flame that fuels good deeds done on behalf of those in need."

A COMPANY WITH HEART

Community service is an American ideal. When French nobleman Alexis de Tocqueville studied American institutions in the 1800s, he was astounded by the willingness of citizens to pitch in and help neighbors in need. "Americans are an unusual people," he wrote. "When they see a problem come up, they immediately form a group or a committee — whatever is necessary to get the job done."

Service is also a Dominion ideal, one rooted deeply in its core businesses — first as a transportation operator, then later as producers and distributors of electricity. For a century, the company has provided public services essential to everyday life. In 1909, employees understood that an inoperable trolley meant the loss of transportation for customers. Today, they know that loss of electricity halts all sorts of crucial activities. "When the lights go out and it is 20 degrees outside, our employees know that it doesn't matter if it is cold — they still have to get out there and get the job done," said Cynthia "Cindy" Balderson, philanthropy manager.

Getting the job done, however, is more than completing the work — it's serving the company's customers under every circumstance when no one else can. "I always felt like I was doing something for the common good by working with a utility," explained Buddy Earley, former general manager of Engineering and Operations for Virginia Natural Gas. "It was something I learned by watching my father, who worked 42 years with the company as a streetcar driver, bus driver, and field supervisor. I started after a military career, and I never thought

I'd find the closeness and camaraderie that I had there, but I was dead wrong. The power company has the same sense of urgency, the same commitment to mission that I'd experienced in the military, and I found that richly rewarding."

The commitment to mission described by Earley works in Dominion's favor by attracting employees who feel the same calling. "I wouldn't mind being on a deserted island with the people I work with," said Tom Chewning, retired executive vice president and CFO and volunteer for numerous community activities, including chairman of the board for U-TURN, Inc., a Christian ministry to young athletes. "Dominion has employees with a lot of different personalities and backgrounds but what's common to all is a high character and value-driven mindset. People like that really do look beyond their own individual circumstances and see the needs of the community and the needs of individuals around them."

A HISTORY OF SERVICE

Where corporate giving was once voluntary, it has become commonplace — even expected — for businesses to have formal volunteer programs that address and meet community needs in sweeping, comprehensive ways. "What may be most original about America is not free enterprise in the business sector, or democracy in the political sector, but the creation of a third great institution that's unique in size and significance — volunteerism in the private sector," said former CEO Bill Berry in a 1986 interview.

The company has made concerted efforts, both small and large, to

Company employees in Virginia Beach, Virginia, participated in the 1985 WalkAmerica for the March of Dimes. While a formal volunteer program was not established until 1984, the company and its employees have been active in community service throughout its 100-plus years. Walks for causes such as breast cancer awareness, Alzheimer's, and leukemia are common ways employees donate their time and money.

meet specific community needs throughout its history. One of the earliest companywide service projects mentioned is from the 1918 *Public Service News*, when employees packed Christmas boxes with food to deliver to needy families during the holiday season. In 1929, *The Vepcovian* highlighted the company's involvement with Richmond's Community Fund, the precursor to United Way. Twelve hundred company employees participated by raising $5,000 collectively to support the agency.

Times of war — from World War II through Korea, Vietnam, the Gulf War, and Iraq — spawned myriad community services and programs. In the 1970s, the focus expanded to include environmental programs throughout the company's service area.

In 2005, Dominion saluted 350 employees and contractors with a patch honoring their fire and rescue volunteerism.

The company's first formal volunteer program was created in 1984, a time when public programs affected by federal spending cutbacks began soliciting the private sector for increased charitable support. The year before, when Bill Berry spearheaded the Richmond Metropolitan Area United Way campaign, he felt that "if we really want a community that is responsive to human needs — needs that we have identified on a local level and given a local priority — it's up to us." Berry brought this idea back to the company and charged the volunteer program with identifying key programs to emphasize throughout the company. Early initiatives included the March of Dimes, mentoring partnerships with schools, and adopting state parks throughout Virginia to help with renovations and maintenance.

Twenty-five years later, the number of programs supported by Dominion has grown exponentially. In 2008 the company's Volunteer Database was implemented, capturing volunteer participation for 17,000 employees scattered over 12 states. Collectively, the

SERVING OUR MILITARY

Dear Editor:

I received the July edition of The Vepcovian *and I want to thank you for sending me this book. I enjoy reading about what my friends are doing back on my old job and wish I could be back there with them. But, as you all know, this is a job that just has to be done. ...*

Edward L. Gibbs, a Richmond transportation employee with the U.S. Army's 100th Battalion, wrote the above letter in 1943, but it could just as easily have come from a serviceman from World War I or the current Operation Iraqi Freedom. That's because Dominion employees have a reputation for jumping in to serve their country — and being served, in return, by their fellow employees left behind. It's one of the best examples of how the One Dominion spirit has prevailed over the last century.

In World War I, employees rallied by sending soldiers care packages and letters, women stepped in to fill vacancies as trolley car operators, and the board of directors authorized supplementing government pay for soldiers to full former compensation.

World War II efforts were more formal, with

Meter reader and Army Reservist Larry Shelton was featured in a 2006 ad thanking him and other employees for their military service. "We are very proud of our colleagues who put their lives on the line," said Hunter Apple-white, director-Advertising & Creative Services.

In September 2008, CEO Tom Farrell (*center*) accepted the Secretary of Defense Employer Support Freedom Award on behalf of Dominion, the highest recognition given to employers for their support of employees who serve in the National Guard and Reserve. The company was one of 15 employers recognized by Employer Support of the Guard and Reserve, an agency of the U.S. Department of Defense, at a ceremony in Washington, D.C. On hand to accept the prestigious Freedom Award for Dominion were (*clockwise from left*) Eric Jones (Petersburg, Virginia), Mike Monfalcone (Richmond), Donald Thomas (Akron, Ohio), George Newsome (Possum Point, Virginia), Bev Robinson (Richmond), and Farrell. Monfalcone, who nominated the company for the Freedom Award, was flown in from Iraq for the ceremony. The company provides a generous military leave policy and also actively recruits returning service members.

the company enhancing support of the war effort by promoting victory gardens, rationing, and underwriting services such as the VEPCO Canteen Corps, which provided meals to troop trains traveling through Richmond. "So far as I have been able to learn the Virginia Electric and Power Company is the only organization in the city which has its own corps," said Captain Nora Blake in a 1945 *Vepcovian* article. "We work at Broad Street every second and fourth Friday nights and will continue to do so until the last troop train rolls by."

Today, Dominion continues to focus on employees called to active duty, with a military leave policy that provides supplemental pay and benefit coverage for up to five years, care package coordination, service member "adoption" programs, support for families of active duty employees, transition assistance to help veterans transition out of the military and back into the workforce; and active recruitment of veterans.

The company also supports employees activated to support natural disasters and border protection with six months of pay and benefit continuation. "Dominion realizes that our employment policies must help those who sacrifice to serve our nation," said Tom Farrell. "While on deployment, our employees should not have to worry about their income and benefits or whether their families will be cared for."

For its exemplary support of war efforts, the company has received several national awards.

Virginia Power employees from the corporate headquarters took to the steps of the Virginia State Capitol in 1991 to show their support for all troops serving in Operation Desert Storm. The company had 21 employees who served in the military reserves and were activated as a result of conflict in the Persian Gulf.

The U.S. Navy commended the company and its employees in 1946 "for meritorious service and outstanding performance rendered beyond normal responsibility during World War II."

The Virginia Committee for Employee Support of the Guard and Reserve (ESGR) awarded the Seven Seals Award to the company two times, in 1991 for the Persian Gulf War (Operation Desert Storm), and in 2008 for Operation Iraqi Freedom. It is the highest award given to publicly recognize American employers providing outstanding patriotic support and cooperation to employees and families of those who have been called to serve.

Also in 2008, Dominion was awarded the Secretary of Defense Employer Support Freedom Award, given to 15 employers nationwide. The company was chosen from a pool of 2,200 nominations submitted from the United States, Guam, Puerto Rico, and the Virgin Islands. "Dominion does so much more than just supplementing pay and deferring employee payment of benefit premiums," said Mike Monfalcone, senior Human Resources specialist in Labor Relations and the Navy Reserve Commander who nominated Dominion for the award. "From care packages and soldier adoption programs to internal recognition for military employees, I thought Dominion needed to be recognized nationally for all it does." ∎

ABOVE: The 1945 VEPCO Canteen Corps in Richmond met all trains carrying soldiers and provided them with refreshment service. *From left, back row*: Phyllis Owen, Mary Bohannon, Mildred Howerton, Nora Blake. *Front row*: Elsie Sergeant, Virginia Rudd, Eunice Sheppe, Ola Anthony, Harriett Owen, Sophie Tyler, Frances Millikan. *LEFT*: Vepcovian "femmes" entertained soldiers on leave at the nightly dances in the Parking Lot Canteen at 7th and Grace Streets in Richmond.

company logged 115,262 volunteer hours valued at $2.3 million, 95 percent of which was recorded from events employees supported after work or on weekends. "These are amazing numbers, and their economic impact on Virginia is significant," said Nikki Nicholau, director of Virginia's Office on Volunteerism and Community Service. "Dominion's excellent reputation of supporting employees in their volunteer efforts makes them an ideal role model for other businesses."

It's no longer enough to promote volunteering; companies like Dominion now encourage and support their employees with training, volunteer time-off, and funding. The company also has a strategic plan in place to keep philanthropy efforts focused. "We try to support as many projects as we can, but we also reserve a portion of our budget for programs that fit with our

Woody Woodson, a Richmond network lineman and a 2007 Dominion Volunteer of the Year, uses his construction skills to refurbish "hogans" at Native American reservations in Arizona and to restore hurricane-ravaged homes in Mississippi and Louisiana. Since creating the program in 1984, Dominion has recognized 249 Volunteers of the Year.

strategic objectives," said Marjorie Grier, director-Corporate Philanthropy.

DOMINION'S HELPING HANDS

In some companies, community involvement and volunteering are ideas pushed down from the top. At Dominion, the opposite is true. While company executives are quite involved in the community and share Dominion's commitment to philanthropy on a personal level, it is the employees themselves who initiate many of Dominion's service activities. Their actions bring to life the original meaning of "philanthropy," which derives from two Greek words meaning "love for mankind."

"Giving back is what we do at Dominion because we are committed to the places where we

live and work," explained Grier. Dominion employees and retirees contribute thousands of hours sharing resources, talents, and knowledge with their communities. They make home repairs for the elderly, refurbish parks, mentor children from elementary to high school, plant trees, build playgrounds, coach sports teams, take mission trips, lead Scouting troops, and participate in walks to raise awareness and funds for many health research organizations. Woody Woodson, a network lineman and a 2007 Dominion Volunteer of the Year, makes annual trips to the Gulf Coast to restore hurricane-ravaged homes. "Out of something as devastating as that hurricane there's plenty of good coming out of it, too," he said. "People go down and become different. As for me, I've found my meaning."

Besides individual pursuits, the company sponsors a series of annual volunteer projects. In recent years, the emphasis has been on environmental clean-up and education. Dozens of communities have benefited through outdoor classrooms, nature trails, and waterway clean-ups. Protecting wetlands in Clover, Virginia; building a greenhouse at an elementary school in Spotsylvania County, Virginia; carving out walking paths at Towpath Trails Park in Northfield, Ohio; and refurbishing areas at Roger Williams Park Zoo in Providence, Rhode Island — all these give employees a variety of hands-on opportunities to help.

THE DOMINION FOUNDATION

In 2008, Dominion complemented its commitment to hands-on service by donating $20 million to charities in five categories of giving: civic and community development, culture and the arts, education, environment, and health and human services. Funding is distributed to projects in states where

In 1991, Virginia Power, WWBT-TV, Ukrop's Super Markets, and the United Way collected 250,000 sweaters through the Sweater Recycling Project, a community-wide drive to provide warm clothing to the elderly, homeless, and other needy people in the Richmond area.

The 1996 Safety Art Contest Calendar featured children's artistic interpretations of everyday safety practices. The purpose of the calendar was to promote the "importance of practicing good safety habits in everything we do."

In 1981, employees such as secretaries Jean Sharp (*left*) and Crystal Hackney (*right*) helped raise $190,000 — a 26 percent increase over the previous year — for Richmond's United Way fund.

Surry Power Station volunteers helped spruce up the playground and classrooms at Smithfield, Virginia's Head Start program in 1997.

Virginia Power volunteers worked at the Central Virginia Foodbank in 1989. *From left*: Mary Jackson, Teresa Mills, Mike Petrochilli, and Linda Bruce.

Since 1988, the Dominion VITA (Volunteer in the Arts) Award has honored dedicated individuals who give their time and talents to ensure that the arts thrive in the Pittsburgh region. Shown is Bill Hall, vice president-Corporate Communications & Community Affairs, presenting Ruth S. Hahn with a 2007 Dominion VITA Award for her work with the Old Economy Village, a historic Pennsylvania site.

ENERGYSHARE

Picture this ... a child sitting at a kitchen table doing his homework while bundled up in his winter coat. For some, it's a chilly reminder that not everyone can afford heat. For others — the unemployed, working poor, and families facing financial peril — it's a grim reality that plays out day after day. Rising out of the need to help those who need it most, EnergyShare was created in 1982.

The program, originally called HeatShare, was novel in that it was one of the first to allow employees and customers to give directly to customers in need. Initially implemented at Virginia Natural Gas (VNG) as a pilot project, HeatShare collected and distributed the funds to those who needed help paying their gas and electricity bills. "We were a little apprehensive about the concept because

Virginia Governor Tim Kaine (*right*) joined Dominion Virginia Power President Dave Heacock at an event in honor of EnergyShare's 25th anniversary. The umbrellas imprinted with the slogan "all seasons ... always there" symbolized EnergyShare's switch to year-round support for customers in need of assistance with energy bills.

other companies had tried it with mixed success," remembered Bill Berry. Those doubts were allayed in its first year, when VNG employees and customers raised more than $28,000 in the pilot program.

In 1983, the program became permanent and was rolled out companywide with a new name, EnergyShare. "The people who have given their support to EnergyShare are the most important part of this program," remarked Jack Ferguson, the company's former president, in a 1986 *PowerLine* article. "People — both customers and employees — have contributed so that others in need can stay warm during the winter. Their generosity is what makes EnergyShare work."

Today, EnergyShare is one of the company's longest running and most successful community service programs. Now a year-round energy assistance program, it offers heating assistance in the cold winter months and cooling assistance in the heat of the summer. Employees donate directly to the fund; customers can contribute with a donation paid through their company bill.

To date, EnergyShare has raised more than $31 million, with 100 percent of donations going

Through the years, EnergyShare's successful ad campaigns have featured the elderly and children, such as this example of people who must bundle up inside to keep warm. *RIGHT*: A 1983 EnergyShare brochure explained the program. *ABOVE LEFT*: The first bill insert to promote EnergyShare.

directly to provide one-time payments of last resort for those who have exhausted other forms of assistance or who do not qualify for help. "We consider EnergyShare the signature program for our company and its customers," said Eva Teig Hardy. "Helping our most vulnerable citizens is foremost in the minds of our employees and customers." ∎

At its 1956 "Report to Top Management" luncheon, the Virginia State Chamber of Commerce recognized VEPCO for its sponsorship of the Jamestown Festival. *From left*: Rex Smith, vice president, American Airlines; Chris Whitman, the Chamber's Richmond Industrial Director; and Erwin Will, VEPCO president. BELOW: *Empires in the Forest: Jamestown and the Making of America* was published on the 400th anniversary of the Jamestown landing. Dominion committed more than $1 million to organizations including The Trust for Public Land, the Jamestown-Yorktown Foundation, and APVA-Preservation Virginia to help preserve the Jamestown site and its legacy.

Dominion operates or locations where it has significant facilities or business interests. "Our presence in the community is felt on a daily basis," said Eva Teig Hardy, former executive vice president-Public Policy & Corporate Communications. "We try to strengthen that presence by being a good neighbor."

Dominion's strategic approach to giving came about when the company acquired Consolidated Natural Gas (CNG) in 2000. Dominion had always been a large community donor, but CNG had a formal giving process in place — an independent foundation to address the company's philanthropic concerns. Dominion adopted the same approach, expanding the foundation to reflect the growing community presence of the company. "Having the Dominion Foundation not only says to the world that our company cares enough about philanthropy to have our own foundation, but it also centralizes our giving efforts," explained Grier. It was one of the many benefits of the merger.

Foundation efforts include the company's matching funds program, which provides a one-to-one match of employee, retiree, and Board of Director gifts to qualified organizations. Employees who serve on the board of a qualified charity or have volunteered substantially on the organization's behalf can have their personal donations matched two-for-one by the company.

CARING FOR CUSTOMERS

The projects Dominion chooses to support demonstrate the company's affinity for its customers. This is especially true for those who need help heating their homes in the winter or staying cooler in the summer. Consequently, resources are set aside annually for special assistance programs such as EnergyShare, a nearly 30-year-old fuel assistance program of last resort for those facing the possibility of not being able to pay their electricity bill, and Fan Care, through which fans are provided free of charge to the elderly poor.

Often, current events dictate the flow of Dominion's philanthropic resources. In 2009, the economic recession caused a spate of job layoffs and business closures across the nation. Rising unemployment and the growing number of uninsured people left many without medical coverage. Rather than spend the $1 million budgeted for the Dominion Day employee recreational events, the company opted to donate the money to free medical clinics throughout its service area.

"Before coming to Dominion, I worked with disadvantaged people who really needed medical attention but could not afford it and had no insurance to cover it," said Leslie A. Krieg, an administrative assistant with Dominion East Ohio's Pipeline

In lieu of Dominion Day recreational events in 2009, employees donated $1 million through the Dominion Foundation to more than 100 free health clinics in the 14 states served by the company. Touring the "Open M" clinic in Ohio were (*from left*): facility director John Moritz, Dominion East Ohio intern Christina Stembridge and president Bruce Klink, and nurse Marol Oddo.

Safety group. "The donation was a wonderful way to give back to the community. Free clinics meet a basic need and have a much higher overall value than recreational activities."

LEADING THE WAY

Because developing strong leaders is a benefit to both Dominion and the community, in 1990 the company created the "Strong Men & Women: Excellence in Leadership" series. "The company has always had an interest in developing solid leadership skills in youth," said Virginia Board, the managing director of Community Affairs & Philanthropy who started working for the company as a high school student in 1969. "Indeed, it is one of the few ways the Dominion of today can ensure the success of the Dominion of tomorrow."

Held in conjunction with Black History Month, the program is more than a diversity program; it is an educational outreach project that has had significant positive influence on the people it has touched. Through the series, the company honors outstanding contemporary role models whose achievements demonstrate that dreams can come true — if matched by equal amounts of desire and hard work.

In turn, biographies of the role models go into creating complementary curricula for public schools, colleges, museums, libraries, churches, and civic groups across the Dominion service area. In 1996, the program was expanded to include a writing contest for high school juniors and seniors as a way to involve them more deeply in the program. Overall, the initial focus was on African-American students, but in recent years students of a number of ethnicities have participated.

"While it was a great and unexpected honor to be chosen, the program's real impact is the example it sets for young people," said Rosalyn S. Hobson, associate dean for graduate studies in the School of Engineering at Virginia Commonwealth University and a 2008 recipient. "When you are young and you see someone accomplish something and you can identify with them, it puts what they are doing in the realm of possibilities. It makes them think, 'One day that could be me.'"

Counted on throughout the community, Dominion and its employees inspire others daily with their "doing well by doing good" approach to business. Serving others is at the heart of everything Dominion employees do, both on and off the job.

Said Cindy Balderson: "At the start of any volunteer project I always think that it's not going to happen, that it's too big or too much. But at the end of the day, after people work hard and give it their best, the job gets done. It's magic to see it all come together." ◆

Strong Men & Women: Excellence in Leadership Series role models are honored with their portraits emblazoned on a commemorative poster. In 2009, the honorees included (*from top left*): Frederick R. Nance, Leland D. Melvin, Matthew Guidry, Ph.D., Dianne Reynolds-Cane, M.D., Sister Cora Marie Billings, RSM, Michael R. White, Vel R. Phillips, Eddie N. Moore, Jr., and Rear Admiral Michelle J. Howard. *TOP*: A poster for the *Strong Men & Women* student writing contest.

SERVICE THROUGH THE YEARS: A TIMELINE

How many different community service projects do Dominion and its employees support? The answer is as varied as Dominion's employees. Service projects over the years illustrate that diversity and creativity are common threads in all that Dominion does.

1918 Virginia Railway and Power Company employees pack Christmas boxes with food to deliver to needy families during the holiday season.

1929 Twelve hundred company employees collect $5,000 for Richmond's Community Fund, the precursor to the United Way.

1933 Employees in the Petersburg-Hopewell district volunteer to raise money to pay all travel and medical expenses for a four-year-old girl with an acute bronchial condition.

1953 The VEPCO Home Services department begins offering demonstrations at the Virginia School for the Deaf and Blind. Frying eggs, learning to use measuring cups, rolling out pie dough, and operating small kitchen appliances are part of the curriculum taught by home economists.

1964 At the Potomac District Headquarters, Vepcovians donate 87 pints of blood in the Alexandria Chapter American Red Cross Blood Drive. The office began contributing in 1953 and has since donated 1,398 pints of blood — or almost 175 gallons — to the effort.

1977 VEPCO sponsors Richmond's largest blood drive, which also features the largest number of donors contributing blood.

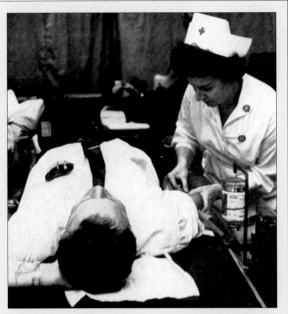

In 1964, R. P. Andrews, assistant general line foreman in the Potomac District, donated a pint of blood through a company-sponsored Red Cross blood drive. In 2009, Dominion employees took part in 30 blood drives for the Virginia Blood Services.

1979 VEPCO employees assist Junior Achievement students in creating their own mock corporations to learn about the free enterprise system.

1985 Employees in the company's Eastern Division Customer Information Center pool their resources to sponsor children at Hope Haven, a home for children without families or who are in crisis.

1986 Dominion raises more money than any other electric utility in the nation for March of Dimes WalkAmerica. More than 8,000 employees contribute $235,000 by participating in the 10K walk.

1993 Dominion offers to tutor students in the Richmond Public Schools, and quickly fills four buses with employee volunteers. The effort blossoms into Lunch Buddies, an ongoing mentoring program that has benefited more than 1,000 students.

1995 Volunteers at the North Anna and Surry Power Stations work with state Boy Scouts of America leaders to help youths earn the Energy Merit Badge.

2001 "It's Electric" kicks off at Innsbrook Technical Center in Glen Allen for the Girl Scouts from the Commonwealth Council of VA, Inc. This educational event teaches Girl Scouts in grades 7 through 12 about how electricity works.

2003 After Hurricane Isabel, Dominion volunteers collect two-and-a-half tons of canned food for the Central Virginia Foodbank. With donations from the Dominion Foundation, volunteers deliver more than 300 Meals on Wheels to individuals isolated by the storm's devastation in New Kent and Charles City counties.

2009 Working with Corporate Angel Network, Dominion offers unused seats on its corporate jets to cancer patients and their families free of charge. ∎

Girl Scouts and Boy Scouts receive patches or merit badges like these for participating in Dominion-sponsored electricity programs.

Richmond Public School students and Dominion tutors enjoy time together in the Lunch Buddies mentoring program, a popular volunteer program since its inception in 1993. Clowning for the camera with their mentees in 1996 were (*left to right*) employees Cindy Davis, Alice Hansbarger, Nathaniel Williams, and Lora Spiller.

Dominion's NedPower Wind Farm partnership with Shell WindEnergy along 12 miles of the Allegheny Front in West Virginia consists of 132 wind turbines capable of producing electricity to supply 66,000 homes and businesses. The turbines are 15 feet in diameter, 335 feet high, and feature blades that spin 100 feet from the ground.

CHAPTER 6

Into the 21st Century

YOU HAVE TO HAVE VISION, you have to be able to see that vision, and you have to be able to change.

TOM CAPPS

retired Chairman, President, and CEO

If Dominion's history was plotted on a graph, the line drawn to represent the first 90 years would depict a slow ascent with occasional peaks and valleys to mark the milestones. The most recent 10 years, however, would be more akin to an electrocardiogram chart, with the line climbing and dipping in rapid succession. That's not to say the company hasn't had direction since the year 2000; on the contrary, Dominion has experienced one of the most focused-but-innovative, risky-but-successful eras in its entire history.

In the span of a decade, the company transitioned from deregulation to re-regulation, from international interests to a "MAIN to Maine" concentration, from an integrated energy enterprise to a streamlined utility with generation, delivery, transmission, storage, and retail businesses. "If we hadn't changed, I think we would have been taken over by somebody," said former CEO Tom Capps.

As the adage goes, the one constant is change. Dominion, however, has another constant: resolve. Translating challenges into opportunities, maintaining a healthy respect for the company's long history of tailoring business to market conditions, and being flexible but decisive have contributed to Dominion's ongoing story of success. As Jack Ferguson, former president of the company, said in 1988:

Goals give direction to our efforts. But they also allow us to change course should conditions change. That's the beauty of goals. They're not commands, they're commitments. They don't determine the future, they mobilize our resources and motivate us to shape the future in ways that benefit our mission.

Commenced in 2008, the 585-megawatt Virginia City Hybrid Energy Center in southwest Virginia will be one of the cleanest power stations of its kind. With an innovative circulating fluidized bed, the station will be powered by coal, waste coal, and up to 20 percent biomass.

A 2001 cartoon contrasts Virginia's relatively smooth preparation for deregulation in 2002 with the state of California's bungled attempt a year earlier. In the following decade, however, electricity rate caps and high wholesale prices kept competitors at bay in Virginia and other states.

FULL SPEED AHEAD

Anyone with a cell phone understands the numerous opportunities for choosing a carrier. What plan works best for your family? Which is cheapest? What company provides the best service, the most options? When the architects of utility deregulation imagined the future, they envisioned a competitive marketplace driven by customer choice. Just as today's consumers can choose their cell carriers or airlines based on individual preferences and needs, so, too, would they be able to choose a utility company to supply their electricity.

Their vision was on the fast track to becoming reality as Dominion Resources entered the new

millennium. Virginia was working toward a 10-year timeline to implement deregulation and competition, and Dominion had positioned itself well. Following the successful merger with Consolidated Natural Gas, Dominion was the nation's fourth-largest integrated electric power and natural gas company. "Bigger is better," said Capps at the time. "The new Dominion Resources will have the scale, the scope, and the skills to be a preeminent leader in the competitive, converged energy marketplace." *Fortune®* magazine agreed, naming Dominion America's second most admired utility in 2000.

On New Year's Day 2002, the future finally arrived. Virginia's electric deregulation plan for generation and the phase-in of customer choice went into effect, with rates capped until July 2007 (and later 2011) to insulate consumers from price and supply uncertainty and to provide time for healthy markets to develop.

Critics feared the plan could spark the same types of problems California had experienced with deregulation. When that state deregulated in 1996, utilities were able to sell electricity to neighboring states at a higher profit. That created a shortage of energy supplies within the state, which led to rolling blackouts and brownouts. Supporters of Virginia's plan, however, believed that California's difficulties were rooted in flaws in the state's deregulation law. Pennsylvania Representative Frank Tulli asserted that his state, after restructuring, was not headed for a California situation, "and from what I have seen in your plan, neither is the state of Virginia," he said in a 2001 speech to Virginia's General Assembly.

Customers were also worried. "I was at a 50th anniversary party for some old friends," said Charles Donato, then manager-Internet Communications, in a 2001 *Connect* article. "The 83-year-old groom stopped me as my wife and I were leaving. He asked, 'Are we going to keep the lights on?' At first I thought he was joking, but then I saw he was sincere. He was really asking for assurance."

Dominion allayed public anxiety by educating its most effective ambassadors — its employees — and deploying them to explain deregulation Virginia-style. "Electricity deregulation is a work in progress," said Eva Teig Hardy at the time. "The initial move to deregulation was prompted by the promise of cost savings, efficiencies, and improved service. Despite the disaster in California, we're

RIGHT: One of the major challenges of creating new energy sources and getting the power to where it needs to go is the placement of transmission lines. Public opposition ("not in my backyard") and environmental, topographic, geographic, and economic constraints also add to the complexity of the challenge.

DOMINION AT A GLANCE

Operating Segment:

DOMINION VIRGINIA POWER

Dominion Virginia Power delivers electricity safely and efficiently to 2.4 million homes and businesses in Virginia and northeastern North Carolina. Of all the company's business segments, this one interacts most directly with customers. Downed power lines, electricity connections, outage repairs, and customer service are part of a day's work for DVP employees.

Business Lines:
- Electric transmission
- Electric distribution
- Energy and related products and services in competitive retail markets

- ◼ Regulated Electric Distribution (Va.) and (N.C.)
- — Electric Transmission Lines (Bulk Delivery)

Does not reflect 1.6 million nonregulated retail customer accounts in 12 states.

As of February 2010

Operating Segment:

DOMINION ENERGY

Dominion Energy is the natural gas-related businesses. This includes exploration and production, natural gas transmission, distribution, storage, exploration and production, and liquefied natural gas (LNG) operations.

Business Lines:
- Natural gas transmission
- Natural gas distribution
- Natural gas storage
- Gas and oil exploration and production; producer services

- — Natural Gas Transmission Pipelines
- — Natural Gas Transmission Pipelines (Partnership)
- ◼ Natural Gas Underground Storage Pools
- ▲ Cove Point LNG Facility
- ◼ Regulated Natural Gas Distribution (Ohio)
- ◼ E&P Producing Area
- ◼ Regulated Natural Gas Distribution (W. Va.)

As of February 2010

Operating Segment:

DOMINION GENERATION

Dominion Generation produces electricity. The company has a fleet of regulated generating stations and also operates a merchant power fleet that supplies the regulated markets in Virginia and wholesale markets in the Midwest and Northeast.

Business Lines:
- Utility power production
- Merchant power production

Operating Segment:

DOMINION RESOURCES SERVICES

Everything that happens behind the scenes to keep the company operating smoothly and efficiently is coordinated and guided by Dominion Resources Services. The services company focuses on providing cost-effective, high-quality business services in ways that are consistent with company operating goals and business plans.

Services:
- Finance
- Accounting
- Budgeting
- Risk Management and Treasury
- Law
- Regulation
- Human Resources
- Information Technology
- Public Policy, Communications and Environmental
- Fleet, Facilities and Supply Chain Management
- Corporate Governance and Shareholder Administration
- Alternative Energy Solutions

Generation Stations in Operation

- ■ Coal
- ■ Hydro
- ■ Natural Gas
- ■ Nuclear
- ■ Oil/Gas
- ■ Biomass
- ■ Wind

New Generation Stations Planned/ Under Development

- ✚ Coal
- ✚ Natural Gas
- ✚ Biomass
- ✚ Wind

Phase 1 in Operation

- ▲ Wind

As of February 2010

"D" IS FOR DOING THE RIGHT THING. "D" IS FOR DOMINION.

In 2003, Dominion kicked off an advertising campaign that focused on the "D" in Dominion. One particular point drove home the belief that "D" is for doing the right thing, something Dominion has practiced for the past 100 years. Dominion understands that in the end, a good reputation, honestly earned, is all that matters. There are no relationships, no public trust, no employee loyalty without it.

In 1970, the company adopted the VEPCO Creed, promising in part:

> TO PURSUE only those objectives that are consistent with the welfare of the public, willingly assuming our share of responsibility as a corporate citizen in the communities in which we operate, cooperating with our industry in research and development projects to solve problems that affect the public welfare, and observing the highest ethical and moral standards.

This ideal was expanded in 1984 when Dominion adopted a code of ethics. "We've always been committed to doing business in accordance with the law and the ethical values of our society," said Bill Berry, chairman at the time. "The new code simply formalizes that commitment and helps us build a solid ethical foundation to guide our organizational behavior."

In the wake of corporate accounting scandals that have erupted with unfortunate regularity in recent decades, Dominion renewed its commitment to ethics in 2007 by formally naming it one of the company's four core values. As stated in *Dimensions 2008: A Report to Stakeholders on Values, Goals*

& Performance: "Doing right — and being perceived to do right — are essential to doing well. Bottom-line results are not the only indicator of performance. Our employees know that businesses do not choose between right and wrong. People do. Individual integrity and behavior are what matters."

That employees believe Dominion strives to do the right thing is reflected in a 2006 employee survey. The poll revealed that 91 percent of Dominion employees surveyed perceived that the organization shows a commitment to ethical decisions and acting with integrity.

"Everybody is on the ethics bandwagon and said, 'Oh, yes, we care about being ethical,' but most people don't care what you say; they care what you do," said Pam Snider, director-Work Force Relations. "Ethics as a core value means living it day in and day out — not just talking about it." ∎

ABOVE: The "Have you seen 'D' today?" advertisements portrayed Dominion as smart, dynamic, and sophisticated. Launched in 2003, the ads communicated Dominion's vision and brand. Interestingly, the "D" symbol is one of a finite number of one-letter symbols used on the New York Stock Exchange. *TOP LEFT*: In 2008, *Corporate Responsibility Officer* magazine recognized Dominion as one of the 100 Best Corporate Citizens among U.S. companies. The list identifies companies with proactive track records of transparency and full public disclosure.

convinced that if deregulation is done correctly, the initial promise will eventually come true. We're doing everything we can at Dominion to make sure we get it right the first time."

"Getting it right" meant staying true to Dominion's vision of building a fully integrated energy company in the Midwest, Northeast, and mid-Atlantic regions – the "MAIN to Maine" expanse, home to 121 million people and 40 percent of the nation's energy consumption. Several key acquisitions were made to bolster the company's generating capabilities. Two were completed previously in 2001: Louis Dreyfus Natural Gas in Oklahoma, which increased the company's natural gas reserves 60 percent to 4.6 trillion cubic feet, and Millstone Power Station in Connecticut, which added two nuclear reactors to the Dominion fleet in a move that also expanded the company's super-regional geographic footprint. Cove Point in Maryland, one of America's largest liquefied natural gas (LNG) facilities, and State Line Power Station near the Illinois-Indiana border were added in 2002. Acquired in 2005 were Kewaunee Power Station, a nuclear facility in Wisconsin, and three fossil generating stations: Brayton Point and Salem Harbor Power Stations in Massachusetts and Manchester Street Power Station in Rhode Island.

Amidst the flurry of acquisitions, the changing marketplace, and an uncertain economic backdrop, Dominion made the strategic move to integrate its electric transmission assets into PJM Interconnection. This regional transmission organization coordinates the movement of electricity through all or parts of 13 states, including Delaware, Maryland, New Jersey, Ohio, Pennsylvania, Virginia, West Virginia, and Washington, D.C. Because Virginia was the fastest-growing state in the PJM system, Dominion's participation would enhance competition in its home state. It also would reduce fuel costs for customers, increase service reliability, and expand access to regionwide economical generation sources.

A SHARPENED FOCUS

By most measures, Dominion appeared settled into a successful business plan by 2005. It served more than five million retail customers in nine states, boasted 28,000 megawatts of generation capability, owned 6.3 trillion cubic feet of natural gas and oil reserves, and was the nation's largest and the world's third-largest natural gas storage operator. Stock share prices were up 14 percent, having hit more than two dozen all-time highs throughout the year. Behind the scenes, however, the company was struggling with its strategic direction.

"During the past few years there have been, in essence, two Dominions," said president and CEO Tom Farrell in a speech at the time. "There has been Dominion Exploration & Production (E&P), and there has been the Dominion wires, pipes, storage, and power generation company. Although we have worked hard internally to become One Dominion, we have never convinced the investment community that the whole of the company is worth more than its individual pieces. In fact, Wall Street has taken the opposite approach."

In 2006, Dominion announced in a bold move that it would sell most of its E&P assets — in essence, a third of the company. It was a significant

After a 7 percent uprate in 2009 at one of its two operational units, Millstone Power Station currently generates enough electricity to power a total of 500,000 homes. The photo shows workers on the turbine floor. Millstone is located in southeastern Connecticut, near New London.

departure from the way the company had done business over the previous few years, but one based on a philosophy of managing for the long-term rather than the short. Because utilities are valued historically for their stability, it was evident that higher earnings based on higher risks in the E&P business were not the best way to create the

Before Dominion announced that it would sell most of its Exploration & Production (E&P) business in 2006, those assets accounted for, in essence, one-third of the company. This offshore oil rig, based in the Gulf of Mexico, was typical of the operation. The sale took place in 2007, and it allowed the company to focus on growing its electric generation and energy distribution, transmission, storage, and retail businesses. Wall Street analysts applauded the bold move.

long-term, stable investment profile that Dominion shareholders preferred.

"When Tom [Farrell] came to me and said, 'I think we're going to sell your E&P business,' it made my heart stop because it was my baby that I'd nurtured for years," said George Davidson, former chairman of CNG and a current Dominion board member. "We talked it through — about analysts' concerns, share price value, and the risky business of it — and when he was finished I said, 'Boy, that sounds good to me.'"

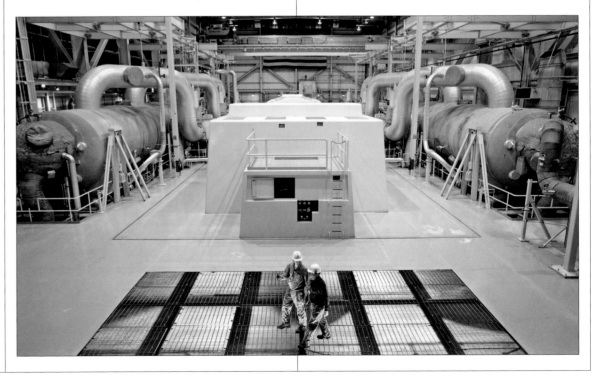

When the sale went through in 2007, it repositioned Dominion from an integrated energy company — with E&P projected to contribute 40 percent of total earnings by 2008 — to one focused on operating and growing power generation and energy delivery, transmission, storage, and retail businesses that include home warranty services, in-home electric and gas line repairs, and energy-related products such as surge protectors and generators. "Dominion after the E&P sale will be a company long on energy infrastructure in some of the most attractive regions in the U.S., but without the cash flow and earnings volatility of the current enterprise," said Mark A. Levin, an analyst with Davenport Equity Research, when the sale was announced.

Narrowing the business model didn't change Dominion's strategy; it simply sharpened the company's focus. It was a "same but different" approach, with Farrell describing it as "being in a position of strength moving to a position of strength." Two years after the sale, the move seemed justified. Dominion's 2009 outlook revealed a lower risk profile while retaining prospects for strong earnings growth.

BACK TO THE FUTURE

For all the talk about deregulation, its success in other industries, and the belief that free enterprise makes for a stronger marketplace, in the end, competition didn't happen in Virginia. "One of the reasons it really couldn't be pulled off is that there was no uniform, national policy," said Paul Hilton, senior vice president-Regulation. "Every state was trying to do its own thing, and we're not a 'state-line' kind of industry. Electricity that goes where it wants to go without any uniformity from a national level is going to go awry."

Project Current Choice.
Giving you a choice in power companies for the first time.

What's Project Current Choice all about?

I can choose my power company.
[X] Yes [ ] No

Project Current Choice, a pilot program that began in 2000, allowed a limited number of Dominion Virginia Power customers to choose among competing electric suppliers. Customers first volunteered to participate, then were solicited by competitive suppliers. If they received an offer they liked, they could switch electricity suppliers. Of the 66,000 who volunteered, 21,507 made the switch. The program ended in 2003.

Competition also failed to materialize because Dominion's rates were already so low, it was nearly impossible for another company to come in and compete. Yet another factor was a growing need to build in-state baseload generation, the best way to keep costs down.

Unlike some states that had rushed into competition, Virginia had the advantage of standing on the sidelines and observing deregulation as it unfolded elsewhere. Competition wasn't faring well; skyrocketing prices were the culprit. For example, Deborah Jackson from St. Louis, Illinois, saw her electricity bill jump from $172 to $600 to $1,000 in the three months after her state introduced competition in 2007. "I'm just working to pay a light bill," she said. In Virginia's neighboring state of Maryland, rates in Baltimore jumped 80 percent in a year. No one wanted the same to happen in Virginia.

"There had been a growing consensus among state legislators on three things," explained Eva Teig Hardy. "First, Virginia needed new power stations to keep rates stable. Second, Virginia consumers needed state oversight of electric rates. Third, any new policy had to maintain restructuring's benefits in promoting utility efficiency and keeping costs stable."

"When we first decided to try deregulation, we worked closely with the General Assembly and came up with a very careful plan that spanned many years and involved slow steps," remembered Hilton. "In hindsight, developing such a cautious plan ended up being a very fortunate thing because it allowed us the opportunity to change our minds."

THE BEST OF BOTH WORLDS

Ultimately, that's exactly what leaders at Dominion did: change their minds. But rather than revert back to traditional regulation, the company worked with the Virginia State Corporation Commission to develop an innovative hybrid proposal. In April 2007, re-regulation was enacted, blending the best of the old cost-of-service regulatory model with lessons learned during deregulation.

The new plan takes into consideration what VEPCO's former chairman, president, and CEO Bill Berry had claimed almost 30 years earlier. "The heart of the old regulatory bargain has collapsed," he said. "Utilities are no longer assured of recovering their costs — even if they result from prudent decision-making. That means the risks of investing under regulation far exceed the potential for rewards. The whole system is out of balance." With competition, he argued that utilities could expect "greater efficiency on the supply side of the business. It will force utilities to become more market-driven, more like other industrial companies."

Besides allowing for continued competition on the supply side of the business, re-regulation includes modifications that provide financial incentives for building critical new power-generating stations, maintaining operational efficiency, and using more renewable energy sources. "We have to have the protection of regulation to assure that we are going to recover what we have invested — it's just too important to the service we provide," Hilton said. "On reflection, we believe it's better for Virginia to build its own resources, not to depend on markets to the north to supply us, in order to have some energy security."

LOBBYING FOR A NATIONAL ENERGY POLICY

Energy security is a perennial topic of concern for utilities, and Dominion has a long history of national activity dealing with the issue. A 1972 report noted that the company was involved in national projects exploring the use of nuclear power as far back as 1957. Dominion was also one of the main utility supporters of the Clean Air Act

amendments of 1990, which imposed strict new regulations on sulfur dioxide and nitrogen oxide emissions to minimize acid rain and ozone formation.

The company began lobbying for a realistic, coordinated national energy policy in 1974 in the midst of the Mideast oil embargo. "The only bright spot in the energy crisis may be that it is serving as a forceful reminder to the public that the nation must have adequate energy and a clean environment, not one or the other," said John M. McGurn, VEPCO's chairman and CEO at the time. "This vital problem cannot be solved in the course of doing business as usual, but rather there must be a coordinated program in which both the public and private sectors are deeply involved and com-

mitted. There is plenty to do and time is short."

McGurn's plan was multifaceted. It called for efficient use of diverse fuel sources, incentives for domestic fuel exploration, prudent drilling for oil and gas, guidelines for eliminating government red tape that delay energy and environmental projects, and increased research and development. He also noted that VEPCO was committed to diversification with generation capabilities fueled by an optimal mix of nuclear, coal, oil, and hydroelectric energy.

Three years later, President Jimmy Carter unveiled his national energy plan, declaring the "moral equivalent of war." His 1977 vision was one of energy independence. It sought to reduce the nation's reliance on imports and move the

Dominion's Political Action Committee (PAC) annually sponsors Dominion Day as an opportunity for members to learn more about the legislative process by attending committee meetings and floor sessions of the Senate and House of Delegates, and by talking with elected representatives. Here, Sherry DeCenso (*left*) and Karen King (*right*) met with U.S. Congressman Robert C. "Bobby" Scott.

Fifty PAC members, pictured on the Virginia Capitol steps, visited individual senators and delegates on Dominion Day in February 2009. The annual event enables constituents, who are also employees and PAC members, to demonstrate their interest in legislative activities and establish a company presence at the General Assembly.

AN EYE ON EXCELLENCE

Hand injuries in generating stations have always been problematic, but in 2005, employee Dave Beckner decided to do something about the number of injuries occurring at Mt. Storm Power Station in West Virginia. Following a process-improvement initiative called Six Sigma, Beckner created a stream-lined safety plan based on data gathered from past accidents. "Before my project, Mt. Storm reported a yearly average of more than eight hand injuries from 2000 to 2003," he said. From 2005 to 2009, the Six Sigma-based plan reduced the station's annual average to fewer than two hand injuries.

No company strives for mediocrity but few are willing to take an honest look at their employees, processes, and products, then make the sometimes difficult changes needed to excel. But with "Excellence" identified as one of Dominion's core values, it made sense to adopt the Six Sigma program companywide in 2000. (Six Sigma originated at Motorola in the 1980s and has been used by about two-thirds of Fortune 500 companies.) Striving to be the best has been an underlying goal throughout the company's 100 years, but creating an environment that welcomed Six Sigma practices and providing employees with the tools and resources to do so has allowed Dominion to implement excellence in a measurable, quantifiable way.

"Six Sigma is driven by a close understanding of customer needs, a disciplined use of data and analysis, and a sharp focus on continually improving the business processes," said Jay Johnson, former Virginia Power president charged with overseeing the implementation. "By changing the way people approach their work, it brings the benefits of quality to the bottom line." The front-line employees, he said, are the ones who make the difference between a good company and a great one.

Dominion was the first company in the energy

At the 2008 International Quality & Productivity Center awards, Dominion placed second in "Design for Six Sigma" for the project "Chesapeake Energy Center Carbon Burnout." Shown with a sponsor of the awards is (*left*) Dave Baxter, manager-Six Sigma for Fossil & Hydro, and (*right*) Rick Boyd, manager-Fuels Operation. *TOP*: Colored belts denote Six Sigma levels of expertise.

industry to apply Six Sigma's process-improvement techniques companywide. Since its inception, the program has produced an astounding $1 billion in savings and has drastically reduced lost-time and restricted-duty injuries at Dominion Virginia Power, cut gas losses at Dominion Energy, slashed water usage at the company's fossil and hydro facilities, and boosted production systemwide at all nuclear stations. "We cannot, however, place only a dollar value on the importance of Six Sigma to Dominion," said Tom Farrell. "Its value transcends a given year's specific dollar savings. It is not just a process; it is part of our culture."

Excellence starts as an attitude, takes shape through action, and ends with superior results — for customers, shareholders, and the company. It bears the stamp of high standards and a commitment to ongoing quality improvement. It shows up when employees don't settle for "good" but reach for "great." As Tom Chewning, former executive vice president and CFO, once said: "The biggest way employees can ensure growth is to perform their jobs in an excellent fashion. They should put themselves in the position of the shareholder and ask, 'If I owned this company, would I do things differently?'" ■

public away from its heavy use of oil toward more use of coal, all in the hope of developing clean and renewable resources and preventing environmental damage. Yet when oil and gas prices eventually dropped, so, too, did the urgency of the issue. "The public and media memory was short, the tyranny of the immediate decisive," said one economist in 1981.

Twenty years later in 2001, just before oil prices once again spiked, Dominion leader Tom Capps spoke to a group of Washington economists about a national energy policy — or lack of it. Comparing energy infrastructure to a "critically ill patient, suffering from clogged arteries, cardiac insufficiency, and self-inflicted wounds," he complained about the inability of Congress to act. "I'm afraid the patient is still sick," Capps said. Further, he believed that the remedy, "a comprehensive strategy for meeting energy needs of American people in a secure and reliable way," was still out of reach.

THE FUTURE OF ENERGY

As the company's centennial year of 2009 approached, the issue of a national energy policy continued to be tossed about in Congress. Tom Farrell likened the problem to a "train wreck." In a 2006 speech, he said: "I am simply convinced that if we do not take steps to shift our nation's energy policy in a meaningful way, the hypothetical train wreck I speak of will come to pass. And the wreckage could include jobs, tax revenues, income growth, energy reliability, national security, and global competitiveness."

Energy policy has consistently appeared to be crisis-driven, assuming a high profile during periods of shortages and price spikes, then receding from the consciousness of policymakers. "The pattern may be changing, however," said Bill Byrd, director-Corporate Public Policy, "with the desire for a lower-carbon future and the recognition that world-wide demand growth has the potential to result in catastrophic price increases."

For the average homeowner, it boils down to "price, availability, and preservation of both our quality of life and our economic growth," Byrd said. "It will be a tall order to keep energy affordable and reliable, and keep homes and businesses comfortable and functioning, while making huge reductions in carbon emissions. A national energy policy cannot ensure that all these goals will be met, but the lack of a coherent strategy, or a poorly designed policy, can virtually ensure that these goals cannot be met."

Interestingly, remedies suggested during the first year of the Barack Obama administration resemble those of Jimmy Carter's day: a realistic, balanced public policy to replace the existing patchwork of different state laws and regulations; diversification of energy sources, including alternative sources; increased reliance on conservation and energy efficiency; greater access to domestic energy supplies; and a business climate conducive to market competition and timely investment in new energy infrastructure. "The energy train wreck that is lurking around the bend is not inevitable," Farrell said. "We have the technology, the resources, and the talent to meet our energy challenges. The key question is, do we have the will?"

DIVERSIFICATION: THE NEW REALITY

The politics of energy may be debated for years before reaching consensus, but there is no denying the facts: In the next 25 years, Virginia demand is

Considering the need for new energy sources in the future, Dominion received an Early Site Permit (ESP) for North Anna Power Station in 2007. The ESP is not a license to construct or operate new nuclear units but provides a 20-year option for Dominion to consider nuclear among other potential generation sources. "It is an important step in ensuring that not only will safe, reliable nuclear energy be available as we plan for future growth, but we will have an electrical generating source that can produce a significant amount of electricity with no greenhouse gas emissions," said Mark McGettrick, now executive vice president and CFO of Dominion.

expected to increase 5,600 megawatts, the equivalent of adding 1.4 million homes to the number the company already serves. The overall demand for electric power in the United States is expected to jump by 50 percent. And the global appetite for power is even greater. Worldwide electricity consumption will double over the same period. How does Dominion expect to keep pace with demand?

"Diversification" has become the new buzzword for the future of energy. On Dominion's Powering Virginia Web site, created to educate the public about what it will take to meet Virginia's energy needs for the 21st century, diversification is presented as the most viable approach to greater energy security. It is an integrated, all-encompassing plan, one that uses a variety of energy sources — coal, nuclear, oil, natural gas, and renewable power — in concert with smarter conservation and efficiency programs. In short, it addresses the key issues of energy production, energy management, and energy delivery.

Virginia is the second largest importer of merchant power in the United States behind California. Without new sources of power generated in the Commonwealth, Virginia will grow increasingly dependent on outside sources — making the state much more vulnerable to price fluctuations. That's why Dominion has pushed to have as many pieces as possible in place. With tentative plans for a new nuclear reactor, building new sources for generation is an obvious solution — but not the only one. Alternative energies, conservation and efficiency

efforts, a diverse mix of fuel sources and operating facilities, and new technologies are all expected to play an increasingly prominent role in providing Americans with the electricity needed to power their lives. "In addition to fuel diversity, we have geographic diversity and exposure to different pricing levels in different wholesale markets," Farrell explained. "Our sales do not depend on a limited number of sites, technologies, or fuel sources, a flexibility that gives our company a distinct advantage. The greater the variety of power sources, the more flexibility we have and the greater our ability to meet our customers' needs."

A COMMON GOAL:
PROTECTING THE ENVIRONMENT

Energy companies, by virtue of their business, are often subject to criticism from environmental groups. Much of this criticism was warranted in the industry's early days, when the nation lacked environmental standards and society paid little heed to environmental impact, stewardship, and the preservation of natural resources. Nevertheless, protecting the environment has long been an

ABOVE: Liquefied natural gas (LNG) operations are part of Dominion's diversification strategy. Dominion Cove Point LNG is conveniently located on the Chesapeake Bay in Maryland so that it can receive shipments of LNG from other countries, store it onshore, then transform it back to gas when needed to meet U.S. demand.
INSET: When a shipment of LNG is received, it is pumped uphill from the pier to storage units until it is needed.

across-the-board priority for all of Dominion's business segments. "I believe Dominion has always tried to do the right thing, but clearly, environmental practices were very different 100 years ago," said Pam Faggert, Dominion's chief environmental officer. "As folks become better informed and more knowledgeable about the environment, we can make better decisions."

As early as the 1930s, VEPCO recognized the need for environmental responsibility. Before building the dam and generating station at Roanoke

DOMINION'S ENVIRONMENTAL STEWARDSHIP

Dominion lives up to its environmental commitments. In addition to stewardship — several examples of which are highlighted here — the company will have spent $3.6 billion on environment controls by 2013 to reduce air and water emissions in its generation business unit. Dominion's capital expenditures for environmental controls total about $200 million per year, and the company spends the same amount annually for environmental operations and maintenance. As the major energy supplier in uniquely beautiful and natural regions, Dominion will continue to protect sensitive habitats and enhance the environmental quality of life for the citizens in the areas in which it does business.

1963 Thousands of pine seedlings are planted at VEPCO's Gaston Hydroelectric Station in Roanoke Rapids, North Carolina, in a reforestation project around the Station's construction site.

J. M. Daughtry, tree supervisor, examined one of the thousands of pine seedlings planted in 1963 at VEPCO's Gaston Hydroelectric Station in North Carolina.

Something as simple as recycling oil that has leaked or would be discarded is environmentally friendly and a money-saver. Mt. Storm's efforts began in 1986 and were soon emulated at other Dominion power stations.

1970 While building Surry Power Station, the company opts to sink the giant reactors 70 feet into the ground to lessen the impact of their height on the landscape.

1973 VEPCO's executive manager of Environmental Control, J. D. Ristroph, invents a fish elevator to protect fish at generating station intakes. Consisting of a heavy steel trough, the elevator transports fish to a flume of running water for transport back into the river away from the intake structure. The device becomes an industry standard, still widely used today.

1978 Company biologists in the Environmental Lab begin catching and tagging lobsters around Millstone Power Station to monitor growth rates, migration patterns, and the general health of the local lobster population. To date, more than 180,000 lobsters have been tagged.

1986 The Mt. Storm Power Station Lube Oil Consumption Task Team creates a plan to recycle leaked or thrown-away lubricating oil. The 11,932 gallons of oil saved amounted to a savings of $40,000 — or 42 percent of the 1986 lube oil budget.

1989 Dominion becomes a founding member of the Avian Powerline Interaction Committee, whose mission is to prevent bird interactions with powerlines.

1990 Dominion celebrates the transformation of a contaminated "Superfund" site near historic York-

town, Virginia, into a modern park featuring three fields for soccer and two softball diamonds. Doing so makes the company one of the first in America to successfully transform a Superfund site into a community asset.

1993 Dominion Transmission provides ongoing funding and other support to the Rocky Mountain Elk Foundation, the Pennsylvania Game Commission, and the Pennsylvania Department of Conservation and Natural Resources for the preservation of elk and deer herds in northern Pennsylvania. Dominion plants a special seed mix along selected areas of the company's pipeline rights-of-way to create safe havens and grazing areas for the elk and deer. Herds have tripled since the program began.

1999 Dominion begins the "Putting Our Energy to Work for the Environment" volunteer initiative. Five hundred employees participate. In the nine years following, more than 5,000 volunteers complete 134 projects, including:

- Transforming 20 acres at the Earth Sangha preserve in the Washington, D.C., area into an arboretum;

- Restoring an urban brownfield and planting a buffer of native vegetation to enhance wildlife habitats for the Save the Bay's National Conference for Coastal and Habitat Restoration in Providence, Rhode Island;

Employees regularly apply their know-how in "Put Our Energy to Work" initiatives. As of 2009, volunteers had pitched in for 10 consecutive years on weatherization and park cleanup projects in Dominion's service areas.

- Creating an "Art Park" in an empty downtown lot in Lima, Ohio; and
- Refurbishing the Pattagansett Girl Scout Camp in East Lyme, Connecticut.

2000 Dominion donates the 477-acre Bear Rocks Preserve in eastern West Virginia to the West Virginia Nature Conservancy. Valued at $1.5 million, Bear Rocks is the single largest corporate gift as well as the largest nature preserve ever donated to the Conservancy. Additionally, Dominion donates $250,000 to the Nature Conservancy of Virginia for land conservation in the Commonwealth.

2003 Dominion partners with the Virginia Institute of Marine Sciences to assist in fish tagging and tracking programs. In the winter months, huge congregations of certain species are attracted to the warm waters in the company's generating station discharge canals. Since the program began, about 10 percent of the fish have been caught again later, some after traveling hundreds of miles. The program provides information that is vital to understanding and managing fisheries.

2007 Cove Point's "green" administration building is completed according to Leadership in Energy and Environmental Design (LEED) standards. Using a variety of environmentally friendly materials and systems, the building uses 32 percent less energy than a typical office building. The building's location was chosen for its minimal impact on surrounding wetlands; 24 percent of the materials were produced locally; 85 percent of construction waste was recycled; and wind power contributes to the building's energy needs.

Dominion Cove Point's "green" administration building in Lusby, Maryland, features a highly reflective/emissive dome-shaped roof with insulated walls and glass windows. The energy-saving LEED design reduces heat loss.

2007 The company reports it has recycled or reduced 1.4 million tons of waste. This includes paper, wood pallets, cardboard, batteries, coal combustion products, used oil and oil filters, scrap metals, and more. It's the equivalent of every resident in Philadelphia recycling 100 percent of his or her garbage.

2008 Dominion's Chesterfield Power Station near Richmond produces artificial gypsum as a by-product of its scrubber, an air pollution control device (officially called a flue gas desulfurization unit) that removes sulfur dioxide from the flue gas.

Dominion is a key sponsor of the Elizabeth River Project's Learning Barge in North Carolina. Launched in 2009, it's a unique solar and wind-powered floating classroom with a living wetland onboard.

The manufactured gypsum is sold to another company that utilizes it in the production of wallboard. These efforts help to conserve natural gypsum reserves and landfill space.

2008 Dominion receives a U.S. Environmental Protection Agency award for its innovative Carbon Burnout (CBO) systems at Chesapeake Energy Center and Brayton Point Power Station. The CBO technology reburns fly ash for energy recovery and, in the process, renders the resulting fly ash suitable for a partial replacement for Portland cement. The CBO operation enables the two generating stations to recover more than 900 million Btu per year of energy that would otherwise be lost with the discarded ash, market the re-burned fly ash to the cement industry, reduce greenhouse gas emissions by several hundred thousand tons annually, and decrease considerably the amount of coal consumed at the stations.

2009 Dominion provides the lead funding for the Elizabeth River Project's Learning Barge, designed to teach students and adults how to help make the Elizabeth River (located in Virginia and North Carolina) "swimmable and fishable" by 2020. ∎

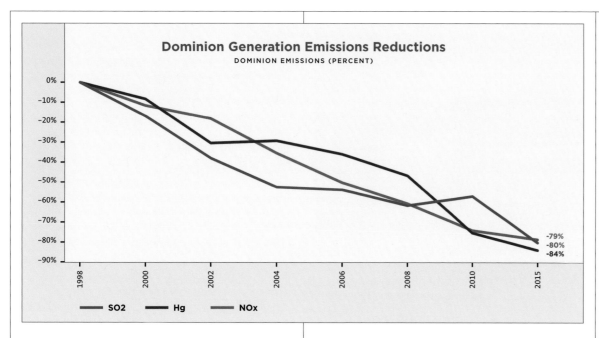

Dominion Generation Emissions Reductions
DOMINION EMISSIONS (PERCENT)

-79%
-80%
-84%

SO2   Hg   NOx

The installation of state-of-the-art emissions control equipment at all of Dominion's fossil fuel-fired electric generating power stations supports the company's commitment to protecting the environment. Since 1998, sulfur dioxide (SO2) and nitrogen oxide (NOx) emissions have decreased by more than 60 percent, and mercury (Hg) emissions have decreased by almost 50 percent — even as electric generating output increased during the same period. In addition, because of its large nuclear fleet, Dominion ranks in the top third of its U.S. peers for the lowest levels of greenhouse gas emissions.

Rapids, North Carolina, the company invested in studies of the Roanoke River to determine the facilities' impact on fish and river flow. In 1935, the company installed fly ash and smoke-abatement equipment to decrease the emissions from its fossil-fuel generating stations. Six years later, the company began monitoring the discharge of heated water that was used as a coolant in its generating stations. The data obtained was instrumental in designing new facilities that minimized harmful effects on fish and aquatic life.

The company formally began to recognize the importance of environmental stewardship in the late 1960s. "It's our world too — so naturally VEPCO is vitally concerned with and giving increasing attention to the environment," stated the company's 1969 Annual Report. In 1970, the same year the federal government created the Environmental Protection Agency (EPA), VEPCO formed its first department of Environmental Control, one of the first utilities to do so. Six employees

transferred from the Power Production department to form the group.

With a formal department addressing environmental concerns, VEPCO was able to better leverage its resources and expertise to create and implement innovative environmental programs to benefit the communities served by the company. It also could take a collective stance on the environmental concerns of the day. One of the first examples is the company's support of the Clean Air Act of 1970, which revolutionized environmental requirements.

Today, Dominion's environmental focus is sharper than ever. Not only does the company strive to comply with all environmental rules and regulations set forth by the EPA and state agencies, it also takes proactive steps to help shape the law in ways that benefit the company and its customers. Perhaps the most notable example is the company's historic 2003 settlement with the EPA governing air emissions. "The EPA decided that coal-fired

industries were not necessarily getting all the permits they needed to control air emissions," Faggert explained. "We disagreed, but we also understood that what they really wanted was elimination of almost all of our air emissions. So rather than contesting it in court like many of our peers, we asked the EPA to sit down with us and resolve the issue cooperatively. It took three years to reach a settlement but it saved us and our customers a lot of money and actually put us ahead of the curve in installing the equipment needed to reduce emissions, which the rest of the industry ended up having to do anyway at a later date." One-third of the cost of a new generating station is for the purchase and installation of environmental equipment.

In another example of Dominion's dedication, a staff of engineers, scientists, and other environmental specialists works closely with the various operating businesses to help ensure full compliance with all environmental laws and regulations. "We provide daily the technical expertise needed to carry out Dominion's environmental initiatives," Faggert noted, adding that the areas around power stations benefit from extensive biological monitoring programs.

According to Faggert, the company's biggest accomplishment during her tenure has been devising cost-effective strategies for achieving compliance and significantly reducing air emissions that offset the accompanying $3 billion price tag. "It was a real challenge to work with our operations team and regulators to figure out the best way to accomplish that. But by doing so, we earned the respect of regulators, and our efforts have paid off in cost savings and environmental results."

The bottom line is that Dominion believes protecting the environment can be achieved in concert with meeting business goals. When the EPA settlement was reached, Wall Street took notice. One analyst commented that it was another example of Dominion being proactive and delivering on its promises.

"It is absolutely possible to meet your business goals while maintaining a commitment to the environment," Faggert said. "Sometimes it may be a little more challenging to figure out how to make it a win-win situation, but fortunately, we at Dominion have gotten pretty good at it."

SUPPLEMENTING WITH ALTERNATIVE ENERGIES

Another boost for environmental protection is developing renewable energies with built-in environmental benefits. While technology has advanced considerably in the past 40 years, it remains expensive and useful in limited applications. Dominion, however, is committed to helping Virginia meet its 12 percent renewable generation target by 2022 and North Carolina's 12.5 percent renewable target

"Green" vehicles made their debut at Dominion in 2009. The first additions to the fleet, two plug-in electric hybrid cars and two hybrid-powered bucket trucks, were part of the company's ongoing efforts to determine the impact of plug-in vehicles on electricity demand.

by 2021. Wind farms that harness wind power, hydropower projects that produce energy from falling water, and biomass stations that burn wood waste to create electricity currently account for a small percentage of the company's fuel mix but have the potential to flourish. However, government projections forecast that renewable energy will rise from today's 6 percent of total production to only 7 percent by 2030.

In 2008, the company began building Virginia City Hybrid Energy Center, an advanced 585-megawatt clean-coal facility in the coalfields of southwestern Virginia. The station will use proven,

flexible clean-coal technology that burns waste coal and as much as 20 percent renewable biomass. Also under development is a pilot carbon storage program at the Brayton Point Power Station in Massachusetts. There, the company is testing cutting-edge technology that converts coal into pipeline-quality natural gas with the potential to separate and capture carbon emissions.

A recent addition to Dominion's renewable portfolio is the NedPower Wind Farm in Grant County, West Virginia, developed in partnership with Shell WindEnergy, Inc. Upon completion the facility will have 132 turbines producing 264

FORWARD THINKERS

There is no crystal ball to reveal the future of the utility industry, but Dominion's forecasters attempt to look ahead as much as possible so the company can position itself accordingly. Historically, these projections, along with those of the U.S. Energy Information Administration, are estimated 20 years ahead. "Ten years is a crucial time frame because it generally takes six to 10 years to build a new power plant," explains Allen Mitchem, manager of Load Research and Forecasting. "It takes forecasting 20 years out to get things in the hopper."

When a planning process is in place, Dominion can aim for a target but have time enough to step away if needed. "If we have made mistakes in our forecast, a good lead time in the planning process lets us cancel projects before we sink too much into them," Mitchem said.

Based on projections by PJM Interconnection, the regional transmission organization, Dominion Virginia Power is expected to experience an increase in customer demand for electricity of nearly 28 percent from 2010 to 2020, making it the fastest growth rate in a 13-state region that stretches from Chicago, Illinois, to Washington, D.C., and the mid-Atlantic. No forecast is ever totally accurate, according to Mitchem. "As trained economists, we try to incorporate as much information as we can about the economy —

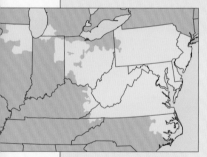

Dominion is a member of PJM Interconnection, the independent organization that operates a competitive electricity wholesale market and manages the high-voltage grid in the areas highlighted.

prices, growth, employment — and build models to provide better forecasts," he said. "We are trying to model human behavior with a set of equations, but it becomes an extremely complex problem when trying to determine what 2.4 million customers are going to do when turning on the light switches." ∎

megawatts of power — enough to serve about 66,000 homes. Dominion also entered into a joint venture with a subsidiary of BP Alternative Energy to develop the 650-megawatt Fowler Ridge Wind Farm in Indiana. And in Hurt, Virginia, Dominion owns one of the largest biomass generating units on the East Coast, generating 80 megawatts of power to serve 20,000 homes.

Although efficiency is not an energy source in itself, the results from maintaining an efficient fleet are evident. Companywide recycling programs and state-of-the-art generation projects such as clean coal combustion processes, the conversion of biomass, coal, and petroleum coke into separate streams of natural gas, and gas-fired generating stations contribute to the company's bottom line and reduce its environmental impact. Currently, slightly more than half of Dominion's 26,000 megawatts of regulated and merchant electric production is fossil-fired. The rest is emissions-free nuclear and hydropower. Consequently, Dominion's carbon intensity, the amount of carbon emitted per unit of energy, is 13 percent below the national average.

CONSUMER CHOICE

Dominion's obligation and privilege to serve its customers will never change. In the coming years, however, that relationship will evolve into a partnership. Energy is well on its way to becoming a

Dominion East Ohio launched a 2009 multi-faceted advertising campaign that included print, radio, outdoor, and online media to increase customer awareness of the Energy Choice program. The ads were part of a cooperative effort among Dominion, the Public Utilities Commission of Ohio, the Ohio Consumers' Counsel, participating suppliers, and others to educate customers on various natural gas supply options.

self-serve industry, where customers have the last say in how much electricity they use — and pay for. Called "demand-side management" (DSM), the idea bundles customer education, energy conservation, and demand-response programs together to figuratively put the power into the customers' hands. "Adding new power supplies and reducing the demand for them are two sides of the same coin," Farrell said. The company currently has 16 DSM programs, all of which feature innovative rate designs and incentives that reward customers for energy conservation.

One of the newest partnerships involves "Smart Grid" technology. In June 2009, Charlottesville, Virginia, became the first "Smart Grid City" east of the Mississippi when Dominion installed Automated

Metering Infrastructure meters citywide. The meters report readings directly to a Dominion database and allow customers to control the amount of electricity used by switching off power at peak times. It is one of the first steps in achieving the futuristic goal of a "Smart Grid," a less centralized, consumer-interactive energy delivery network. "Customers won't have to call us anymore," Farrell said. "They won't have to poke around in the dark with a flashlight trying to find the phone number and phone book. The meter will 'talk back' to us and tell us when they are out of power. The technology gives us constant information so we can give our customers more information."

Yet for all the innovations that Dominion puts into place to conserve energy and maximize efficiency, only the consumer can reduce consumption. Given the responsibility and resources, consumers are expected to reduce their consumption by 10 percent over the next 12 years, as compared to 2006.

A LEGACY OF SERVICE

What does the future hold for Dominion? No one can say with certainty what the stock market and economy will do, even in the near term. Company forecasters can predict 20 years out at best, but even so, the projections merely give the company a target to aim for, not a clearly lit path to the future.

Still, Dominion has the advantage of hindsight to navigate the uncertainties. Said Farrell, "All of what we do here, and the successes we currently enjoy, are built on generations of success in the past." Strong and smart after 100 years of thriving in the utility industry, Dominion is prepared for the interesting, challenging, and complicated journey that lies ahead. ◆

Compact fluorescent lightbulbs (CFLs) produce the same amount of visible light as traditional incandescent bulbs, but they use up to 75 percent less energy and can last 10 times longer. In 2007, Dominion partnered with Home Depot to provide customers with savings of $1.50 on each CFL and $3 on multi-packs. Buyers purchased 3.8 million bulbs in two years, representing a savings of $140 million over the life of the CFL bulbs — enough to provide power to 72,000 Virginia homes for a year.

THE POWER BEHIND DOMINION

ELECTRIC GENERATION

Dominion has operated dozens of generating stations over the years. Some have been retired, others sold. Currently, Dominion's generating facilities produce more than 27,500 megawatts of efficient electric power using a variety of energy sources. With fossil fuel, renewable energy, nuclear, and hydroelectric generating stations all connected through an extensive network of transmission lines, Dominion features a diverse portfolio of energy sources.[1]

STATION	PLACED INTO SERVICE	COMMERCIAL STATUS	LOCATION	FUELS BURNED[3]
Kewaunee	1974	In service	Carlton, Wis.	Uranium
Millstone (Unit 2)	1975	In service	Waterford, Conn.	Uranium
Millstone (Unit 3)	1986	In service	Waterford, Conn.	Uranium
North Anna (Unit 1)	1978	In service	Mineral, Va.	Uranium
North Anna (Unit 2)	1981	In service	Mineral, Va.	Uranium
Surry (Unit 1)	1972	In service	Surry, Va.	Uranium
Surry (Unit 2)	1973	In service	Surry, Va.	Uranium
Altavista	1992	In service	Altavista, Va.	Coal/Sawdust
Bath County (Units 1-6)	1985	In service	Warm Springs, Va.	Water
Bear Garden	(under construction)		New Canton, Va.	Gas
Bellemeade CC	1991	In service	Richmond, Va.	Gas/Oil
Brayton Point (Unit 1)	1963	In service	Somerset, Mass.	Coal
Brayton Point (Unit 2)	1964	In service	Somerset, Mass.	Coal
Brayton Point (Unit 3)	1969	In service	Somerset, Mass.	Coal
Brayton Point (Unit 4)	1974	In service	Somerset, Mass.	Oil/Gas
Bremo (Units 3)	1950	In service	Bremo Bluff, Va.	Coal
Bremo (Unit 4)	1958	In service	Bremo Bluff, Va.	Coal
Chesapeake (Unit 1) (formerly Portsmouth)	1953	In service	Chesapeake, Va.	Coal/Oil
Chesapeake (Unit 2)	1954	In service	Chesapeake, Va.	Coal/Oil
Chesapeake (Unit 3)	1959	In service	Chesapeake, Va.	Coal/Oil
Chesapeake (Unit 4)	1962	In service	Chesapeake, Va.	Coal/Oil
Chesapeake CT (Units 1, 2, 4, 6-10)	1967-1969	In service	Chesapeake, Va.	Oil
Chesterfield (Unit 3)	1952	In service	Chester, Va.	Coal/Oil
Chesterfield (Unit 4)	1960	In service	Chester, Va.	Coal/Oil
Chesterfield (Unit 5)	1964	In service	Chester, Va.	Coal/Oil
Chesterfield (Unit 6)	1969	In service	Chester, Va.	Coal/Oil
Chesterfield CC (Unit 7)	1990	In service	Chester, Va.	Oil/Gas
Chesterfield CC (Unit 8)	1992	In service	Chester, Va.	Oil/Gas

Kewaunee

Bath County

Brayton Point

STATION	PLACED INTO SERVICE	COMMERCIAL STATUS	LOCATION	FUELS BURNED[3]
Clover (Unit 1)	1995	In service	Clover, Va.	Coal
Clover (Unit 2)	1996	In service	Clover, Va.	Coal
Cushaw (Units 1–5)	1930	In service	Big Island, Va.	Water
Darbytown CT (4 units)	1990	In service	Richmond, Va.	Gas/Oil
Elwood CT (Units 1–4)	1999	In service	Elwood, Ill.	Gas
Elwood CT (Units 5–9)	2001	In service	Elwood, Ill.	Gas
Elizabeth River CT (Units 1–3)	1992	In service	Chesapeake, Va.	Gas/Oil
Fairless Works CC (Units 1–2)	2004	In service	Fairless Hills, Pa.	Gas
Fowler Ridge Wind Farm	2009	In service	Benton Co., Ind.	Wind
Gaston (Units 1–4)	1963	In service	Roanoke Rapids, N.C.	Water
Gordonsville CC (Units 1–2)	1994	In service	Gordonsville, Va.	Gas/Oil
Gravel Neck CT (Units 1–2)	1970	In service	Surry, Va.	Oil
Gravel Neck CT (Units 3–6)	1989	In service	Surry, Va.	Gas/Oil
Hopewell	1992	In service	Hopewell, Va.	Coal
Kitty Hawk CT (Units 1–2)	1971	In service	Kitty Hawk, N.C.	Oil
Ladysmith CT (Units 1–5)	2001–2009	In service	Ladysmith, Va.	Gas/Oil
Low Moor CT (Units 1–4)	1971	In service	Covington, Va.	Oil
Kincaid (Unit 1)	1967	In service	Kincaid, Ill.	Coal
Kincaid (Unit 2)	1968	In service	Kincaid, Ill.	Coal
Manchester Street CC (Units 9–11)	1995	In service	Providence, R.I.	Gas/Oil
Mecklenburg (Units 1–2)	1992	In service	Clarksville, Va.	Coal
Morgantown	1992	In service	Morgantown, W. Va.	Coal
Mt. Storm (Unit 1)	1965	In service	Mt. Storm, W. Va.	Coal
Mt. Storm (Unit 2)	1966	In service	Mt. Storm, W. Va.	Coal
Mt. Storm (Unit 3)	1973	In service	Mt. Storm, W. Va.	Coal
NedPower (Phase 1)	2008	In service	Mt. Storm, W. Va.	Wind
North Branch	1992	In service	Bayard, W. Va.	Coal
Northern Neck CT (Units 1–4)	1971	In service	Warsaw, Va.	Oil
Pittsylvania	1994	In service	Hurt, Va.	Biomass
Possum Point (Unit 3)	1955	In service	Dumfries, Va.	Gas/Coal/Oil
Possum Point (Unit 4)	1962	In service	Dumfries, Va.	Gas/Coal/Oil
Possum Point (Unit 5)	1975	In service	Dumfries, Va.	Oil
Possum Point CC (Unit 6)	2003	In service	Dumfries, Va.	Gas/Oil
Possum Point CT (Units 1–6)	1968	In service	Dumfries, Va.	Oil
Remington CT (Units 1–4)	2000	In service	Remington, Va.	Gas/Oil
Roanoke Rapids (Units 1–4)	1955	In service	Roanoke Rapids, N.C.	Water
Rosemary CC	1990	In service	Roanoke Rapids, N.C.	Gas/Oil
Salem Harbor (Unit 1)	1951	In service	Salem, Mass.	Coal

Bremo

Portsmouth

Chesapeake

STATION	PLACED INTO SERVICE	COMMERCIAL STATUS	LOCATION	FUELS BURNED[3]
Salem Harbor (Unit 2)	1952	In service	Salem, Mass.	Coal
Salem Harbor (Unit 3)	1958	In service	Salem, Mass.	Coal
Salem Harbor (Unit 4)	1971	In service	Salem, Mass.	Oil
Sidney A. Murray, Jr. Hydroelectric Station[2]	1990	In service	Vidalia, La.	Hydro
Southampton	1992	In service	Southampton, Va.	Coal
State Line (Unit 3)	1955	In service	Hammond, Ind.	Coal
State Line (Unit 4)	1962	In service	Hammond, Ind.	Coal
Yorktown (Unit 1)	1957	In service	Yorktown, Va.	Coal/Oil/Gas
Yorktown (Unit 2)	1959	In service	Yorktown, Va.	Coal/Oil
Yorktown (Unit 3)	1974	In service	Yorktown, Va.	Oil /Gas
Virginia City Hybrid Energy Center	(under construction)		Virginia City, Va.	Coal/Biomass
Millstone (Unit 1)	1970	Retired	Waterford, Conn.	Uranium
Alexandria (Unit 1-3)	1937-1944	Retired	Alexandria, Va.	Coal
Bell Isle Power Station (Units 1-5)	1914	Retired	Richmond, Va.	Water
Bremo (Units 1-2)	1931	Retired	Bremo Bluff, Va.	Coal
Charlottesville	1923	Retired	Charlottesville, Va.	Coal
Chesapeake CT (Units 3, 5)	1967-1969	Retired	Chesapeake, Va.	Oil
Chesterfield (Unit 1)	1944	Retired	Chester, Va.	Coal/Oil
Chesterfield (Unit 2)	1949	Retired	Chester, Va.	Coal/Oil
Embrey Power Station (Units 1-3)	1912-1926	Retired	Fredericksburg, Va.	Water
Hampton (Units 1-2)	1921	Retired	Hampton, Va.	Coal
Hampton (Unit 3)	1936	Retired	Hampton, Va.	Coal
Hampton (Unit 4)	1944	Retired	Hampton, Va.	Coal
Harvell Power Station (Units 1-2)	1922	Retired	Petersburg, Va.	Water
Locks Power Station (Units 1-4)	1907-1930	Retired	Petersburg, Va.	Water
Manchester Power Station	1925	Retired	Richmond, Va.	Water
Possum Point (Unit 1)	1948	Retired	Dumfries, Va.	Coal/Oil
Possum Point (Unit 2)	1951	Retired	Dumfries, Va.	Coal/Oil
Reeves Avenue (Units 1-5)	1907	Retired	Norfolk, Va.	Coal
Reeves Avenue (Unit 6)	1941	Retired	Norfolk, Va.	Coal
Reeves Avenue (Unit 7)	1951	Retired	Norfolk, Va.	Coal
Ronceverte (Units 1-2)	1920	Retired	Ronceverte, W. Va.	Coal
12th Street (Units 1-7)	1903-1940	Retired	Richmond, Va.	Coal/Oil
12th Street (Units 1-9) A.C. Units	1903-1935	Retired	Richmond, Va.	Water
12th Street (Units 1-9) D.C. Units	1900-1926	Retired	Richmond, Va.	Water
Armstrong CT (Units 1-4)	2002	Sold	Shelocta, Pa.	Gas/Oil
Bayonne Enron Cogeneration	1988	Sold	Bayonne, N.J.	Gas

Clover

Ladysmith

Mt. Storm

STATION	PLACED INTO SERVICE	COMMERCIAL STATUS	LOCATION	FUELS BURNED[3]
Belize Electric Company, Ltd.	1995	Sold	Benque Viejo del Carmen, Belize	Hydro
Central Termica Alto Valle	1968	Sold	Buenos Aires, Argentina	Gas
Chalk Cliff	1990	Sold	Kern County, Calif.	Gas
Clear Lake Enron Cogeneration	1984	Sold	Pasadena, Texas	Gas
Corby	1994	Sold	Northamptonshire, U.K.	Gas
COSO BLM Geothermal	1988	Sold	Ridgecrest, Calif.	Geothermal
Egenor, S.A.	1958–1990	Sold	Lima, Peru	Hydro/Gas/Oil
Empresa Electrica Corani, S.A.	1966	Sold	Cochabamba, Bolivia	Hydro
Hidroelectrica Cerros Colorados	1978	Sold	Buenos Aires, Argentina	Hydro
Middle Falls	1989	Sold	Washington, N.Y.	Hydro
NAVY II Geothermal	1989	Sold	Inyo County, Calif.	Geothermal
New York State Dam	1990	Sold	Cohoes, N.Y.	Hydro
Pleasants CT (Units 1–2)	2002	Sold	St. Mary's, W. Va.	Gas/Oil
Rumford	1990	Sold	Rumford, Maine	Coal
San Joaquin	1990	Sold	Stockton, Calif.	Gas
SEGS VII	1988	Sold	Kramer Junction, Calif.	Solar/Gas
Sissonville	1990	Sold	Potsdam, N.Y.	Hydro
Texas City Enron Cogeneration	1987	Sold	Texas City, Texas	Gas
Troy CT (Units 1–4)	2002	Sold	Luckey, Ohio	Gas/Oil
Warrensburg	1988	Sold	Warrensburg, N.Y.	Hydro

[1] *Information based on corporate documents and employee memories.*
[2] *Dominion Capital currently owns a 25% limited partnership interest.*
[3] *Fuels burned since commissioning.*

Possum Point

Reeves

GAS STORAGE AND PRODUCTION

Complementing its generation portfolio, Dominion is the largest operator of gas storage in North America, with almost 2,000 storage wells, approximately 349,000 acres of operated leaseholds, 20 storage pools, 134 compressor stations producing more than 747,000 in horsepower, and 12,000 miles of transmission, gathering and storage pipeline. Its Exploration and Production (E&P) business produced 52.3 billion cubic feet of natural gas equivalents in 2009, with reserves of 1.3 trillion cubic feet from 9,830 producing wells in the Appalachian Basin. In the same year, Dominion drilled 307 wells — without ever hitting a dry hole.

The Oakford Compressor Station in Pennsylvania stores natural gas in two formations, the Murrysville and the Fifth Sand.

POOL NAME	LOCATION	TOTAL OPERATED WITH NATIVE GAS (BCF)	DOMINION OWNED WITH NATIVE GAS (BCF)
Bridgeport	W.Va.	8	8
Fink-Kennedy/Lost Creek	W.Va.	166	166
Racket Newberne	W.Va.	8	8
Ellisburg	Pa.	98	38
Greenlick	Pa.	56	56
Harrison	Pa./N.Y.	34	17
Leidy-Tamarack	Pa.	118	31
North Summit	Pa.	23	23
Oakford Murrysville	Pa.	111	56
Oakford Fifth Sand	Pa.	21	11
Sabinsville	Pa.	36	36
Sharon	Pa.	5	5
South Bend	Pa.	17	17
Tioga	Pa.	36	20
Woodhull	N.Y.	36	36
Quinlan	N.Y.	8	8
Chippewa	Ohio	11	11
Columbiana	Ohio	3	3
Gabor	Ohio	4	4
Stark-Summit	Ohio	151	151

A typical wellhead, where natural gas is injected into and withdrawn from underground storage.

TIMELINE

1795 Dominion's corporate ancestry can be traced to the Upper Appomattox Company, which was organized to improve navigation and commercial development on the James River and its tributaries, including canal operation to secure water rights to the river.

1884 Richmond grants a franchise to Virginia Electric Light and Power Company to provide light and power. The Electric Company of Virginia is incorporated to provide commercial lighting to downtown Norfolk, Virginia. Both companies are part of Dominion's corporate ancestry.

1887 Frank Sprague successfully electrifies the Richmond Union Passenger Railway Company, one of VEPCO's predecessor companies.

1909 On June 29, Virginia Railway and Power Company (VR&P) is formed as a result of a merger between three separate street railways in Richmond: the Richmond Traction Company, the Virginia Passenger and Power Company, and the Richmond Passenger and Power Company.

1911 The Norfolk and Portsmouth Traction Company, a combination of several traction, power, and gas companies, merges into VR&P, allowing VR&P to enter the electric and natural gas distribution markets in the Tidewater area of Virginia.

1915 VR&P forms a benefit association in Richmond that offers members per diem benefits during disability; upon death, the member's beneficiary receives $1 for each member in the association.

1916 The first unit at Reeves Avenue station in Norfolk goes into operation. General Safety Committee, the first general committee of its kind for a Virginia industrial organization, is created by VR&P.

1920 The first transmission line between Norfolk and Richmond goes into operation.

1924 The Virginia State Corporation Commission becomes the company's state regulatory authority.

1925 A syndicate formed by Stone & Webster purchases VR&P and forms Engineers Public Service Company to manage VR&P. Spotsylvania Power Company of Fredericksburg merges with VR&P, and the company's name is changed to Virginia Electric and Power Company (VEPCO). VEPCO begins to sell large and small appliances.

1927 The Norfolk Railway and Light Company merges into VEPCO, expanding the company's presence in the Tidewater region. During the year, VEPCO also purchases several small companies and distribution systems in northeastern North Carolina. A major expansion is completed at Reeves Avenue Power Station. The company also forms the VEPCO Employee Benefit Association, which remains the primary source of benefits until 1945.

1933 VEPCO institutes the 40-hour work week, five years before the Fair Labor Standards Act made it law.

1936 VEPCO formally creates an Industrial Development department to coordinate economic development initiatives throughout the company's service area.

1937 The Independent Organization of Employees becomes the first collective bargaining unit to represent company employees.

1940 The Securities and Exchange Commission brings proceedings against Engineers Public Service Company (VEPCO's holding company), and in 1942 orders a divestiture of all its transportation and gas companies.

1944 VEPCO merges with the Virginia Public Service Company, more than doubling the company's service area and making it one of the largest electric utilities in the nation. Chesterfield Power Station is completed.

1945 VEPCO implements a retirement plan, group insurance, and hospitalization. The benefits replace the VEPCO Employee Benefit Association.

1947 Engineers Public Service Company dissolves, and VEPCO becomes an independent, publicly owned utility with 450,000 electric and gas customers and 11,000 stockholders. In the reorganization, VEPCO sells its trolley business to the Virginia Transit Company.

1948 Possum Point Power Station goes into operation with a 60,000-kilowatt unit.

1953 The Portsmouth Power Station (today's Chesapeake Energy Center) begins operation with a 90,000-kilowatt unit. The U.S. Supreme Court rules in favor of VEPCO building a hydroelectric power plant on the Roanoke River in North Carolina.

1955 VEPCO completes the Roanoke Rapids Hydroelectric Plant, the company's largest hydroelectric plant at the time with a generating capacity of 104 megawatts.

1956 VEPCO joins three other southeastern utilities to construct a prototype nuclear reactor in Parr Shoals, South Carolina.

1957 Yorktown Power Station begins operation.

1958 The Gold Medallion Home Program is introduced to promote better wiring, lighting, and the use of electrical appliances. Its goal is to help customers "Live Better Electrically."

1963 The company begins offering its employees a savings plan.

1964 VEPCO becomes the first utility to sell commercial paper (a short-term promissory note) and in 1977 becomes the first utility to do so without a broker.

1965 VEPCO constructs the innovative Mt. Storm mine-mouth generating station in West Virginia. The company also develops the nation's first 500,000-volt transmission system, beginning at Mt. Storm, to reduce coal transportation costs and transport electricity to major load areas in central and northern Virginia.

1968 VEPCO begins installing underground electric distribution lines for residential customers. This technical innovation becomes standard for newly developed residential areas. The company also authorizes three major construction projects: a third addition to the Mt. Storm mine-mouth station, a second nuclear generating station at North Anna Power Station, and the construction of a pumped-storage facility in Virginia's Marble Valley, which later moves to Bath County when the original site is deemed unsuitable by geologists.

1970 The company becomes the first utility company to implement a department of Environmental Control. Six employees transfer from the Power Production department to form the group.

1971 VEPCO receives national recognition for its environmental efforts in cooling water at its Chesterfield Power Station. The company is named "Utility of the Year" by *The EL&P (Electric Light & Power) Gazette*. Mary Fray, a housewife and activist from Culpeper, Virginia, becomes the company's first female board member.

1972 Surry Power Station, the company's first nuclear power generator, comes online, accounting for 25 percent of VEPCO's energy production.

Company linemen become the first approved in the industry to bare-hand above-ground 500-kv transmission lines. Special suits that allow the electric current to run through them permit the linemen to work on energized circuits.

1973 The company becomes the first utility to issue short-term, tax-exempt pollution-control bonds through local industrial development or similar agencies to achieve lower than corporate rates.

1977 An extremely cold winter forces the company to implement a series of rolling blackouts. It is the first time in VEPCO's history that the company cannot provide enough power to meet demand. The company also cancels construction of Surry nuclear Units 3 and 4.

1978 North Anna Power Station, the company's second nuclear generator, begins commercial operation.

1979 Oil shortages and rising costs cause energy prices to rise and prompt VEPCO to initiate one of the largest oil-to-coal conversion programs in the nation. The company installs the first computerized Supervisory Control and Data Acquisition (SCADA) system to operate power lines and control circuit breakers.

1980 VEPCO becomes the first utility to offer its customers the opportunity to purchase the company's common stock using monthly coupon payments. At the end of the first 12-month period, VEPCO issues customers 544,163 shares of common stock valued at more than $6 million.

1981 The company takes its gas division and forms Virginia Natural Gas. The company's president, Bill Berry, introduces the notion of competition to the utility industry.

1982 VEPCO establishes the HeatShare program (renamed EnergyShare in 1983) to help customers in need pay winter heating bills. Company employees also vote 2-to-1 for no union representation of salaried employees. At the time, it is the second-largest white collar union election in the history of the electric utility industry.

1983 On May 19, Dominion Resources, Inc., is formed as a holding company, and VEPCO becomes its largest subsidiary. VEPCO implements the Customer Assisted Restoration of Service program, an automated outage reporting system.

1985 VEPCO changes its operating names to Virginia Power, North Carolina Power, and West Virginia Power, and implements a new logo and identity program, along with a new logo for Dominion Resources. VEPCO's Bath County Station, the nation's largest pumped storage hydroelectric generating station, begins commercial operations with a generating capacity of 2.7 gigawatts. Dominion Resources forms Dominion Capital, Inc., a financial services company and Dominion Energy, Inc., an independent energy company.

1986 Virginia Power establishes the nation's first licensed aboveground facility to store spent nuclear fuel. Dominion Resources sells West Virginia Power. The Virginia State Corporation Commission rules that Dominion Resources and its non-utility subsidiaries remain financially, commercially, and operationally separate from the company's regulated electric utility franchise. Dominion Resources forms Dominion Lands, Inc., to oversee the company's land holdings and invest in real estate development.

1987 Dominion Energy adds oil and gas exploration to its business pursuits.

1988 Virginia Power enters the competitive bidding market and seeks to purchase 1,750 megawatts of merchant generating capacity.

1989 President George H.W. Bush presents the President's Volunteer Action Award to the Virginia Power Volunteer Program.

1990 The country's first combined-cycle generating unit goes into operation at Chesterfield Power Station. Dominion Resources sells its Virginia Natural Gas subsidiary to Consolidated Natural Gas (CNG).

1992 The company creates "America's Utility Fund," the first mutual fund that invests in utility stocks, and offers the investment to customers through their electric bills.

1993 Dominion Energy plunges into the foreign energy market with the purchase of a 98-megawatt generating plant in southwest Argentina, and later purchases additional generating assets in Bolivia.

1994 Dominion Resources prevails in a court battle that gives it ultimate authority over its regulated subsidiary, Virginia Power. The ruling broadens the company's corporate vision and reinforces its obligation to serve both customers *and* shareholders.

1995 Clover Power Station, the company's first generating facility to be built in recent years, begins operation with a generating capacity of 930 megawatts. Dominion also acquires natural gas and oil assets located in the Appalachian Basin.

1997 Dominion acquires East Midlands Electricity, a U.K. power company, and sells it 18 months later. VEPCO forms VPS Communications to expand its telecommunications business, and in 2000 transfers these operations to the holding company to create Dominion Telecom.

1999 Virginia Governor Jim Gilmore signs into law legislation establishing a detailed plan to restructure the electric utility industry in Virginia. The plan calls for deregulation of generation by 2002, when customers would have the right to choose their energy supplier. Dominion sells its South American generating assets.

2000 Dominion Resources merges with CNG, one of the nation's largest natural gas companies. As a result, Dominion splits into three different operating units: Dominion Delivery, Dominion Energy, and Dominion Exploration & Production, and establishes a service company to provide financial and administrative support to the units.

2001 Dominion acquires Louis Dreyfus Natural Gas in Oklahoma and Millstone Power Station in Connecticut.

2002 Dominion acquires Cove Point liquefied natural gas facility in southern Maryland and State Line Power Station near the Illinois-Indiana border.

2003 Hurricane Isabel hits Virginia and the Atlantic Coast. During Isabel, more than 1.8 million Dominion electric customers are without power. To aid in the restoration effort, Dominion initially assembles a workforce of 7,000. Ultimately, more than 12,000 people contribute to the effort, restoring power after two weeks of around-the-clock effort. After three years of negotiations, Dominion agrees on an historic settlement with the EPA in regard to air emissions.

2004 Devil's Tower, the world's deepest spar platform and the first such deepwater property operated by Dominion, begins operation in the Gulf of Mexico.

2005 Dominion defines its core values: Safety, Ethics, Excellence, and One Dominion (teamwork).

With almost 96 years of service behind it, the company identifies the values that have kept Dominion a successful business. The company also acquires three New England power plants — Brayton Point, Manchester, and Salem Harbor — and Kewaunee Power Station in Wisconsin.

2007 Dominion sells most of its natural gas and oil exploration properties as part of a strategic realignment to focus on its core business. The company begins building Virginia City Hybrid Energy Center, an advanced 585-megawatt clean-coal facility in the coalfields of southwestern Virginia. In April, re-regulation is enacted, blending the best of the old cost-of-service regulatory model with lessons learned during deregulation.

2008 Dominion begins development of a wind power facility in Grant County, West Virginia, to add to its alternative energy portfolio. The company also acquires a 50 percent interest in the 650-megawatt Fowler Ridge Wind Farm in Indiana.

2009 In June, Charlottesville, Virginia, becomes the first "Smart Grid City" east of the Mississippi when Dominion installs Automated Metering Infrastructure meters citywide.

2010 Dominion sells Dominion Peoples, its Pennsylvania natural gas distribution company, in a strategic move to reduce debt. ■

SELECTED BIBLIOGRAPHY

This bibliography is not a complete record of all works and sources consulted. It indicates the substance and range of reading upon which the ideas in this book were formed. Web sites were accessed at various times throughout 2009. The book is also based in large part on the author's interviews with employees and retirees, who are listed in the Acknowledgments.

DOMINION RESOURCES, INC. AND PREDECESSORS: PUBLICATIONS AND DOCUMENTS

A Half Century of Progress. Virginia Electric and Power Company. Richmond: 1959.

Capps, Thos. E. "Why WE Need a National Energy Policy." Photocopied speech. May 24, 2004.

"Chronological Corporate Chart: Virginia Electric and Power Company." Internal chart. Jan. 1, 1937.

Connect (2005–2008). Dominion Resources, Inc.

Connect Today (2005–2009). Dominion Resources, Inc.

Current News (1970–1995). Virginia Electric and Power Company.

Dimensions 2008: A Report to Stakeholders on Values, Goals & Performance. Richmond: Dominion Resources, Inc., 2008.

Dominion Resources, Inc. Annual Reports (1985–2008).

Dominion Resources, Inc. www.dom.com.

"Employee Handbook." VEPCO: circa 1980s.

"Energy Services/Customer Contracts Representative Development Program: Economic Development Program." Company report, 1982.

Farrell II, Thomas F. "A Train Wreck Waiting to Happen?" Photocopied speech. World Affairs Council, Richmond, Va., Sept. 14, 2006.

Farrell II, Thomas F. "Energy and Its Impact on Economic Development." Photocopied speech. Virginia Economic Development Association. Staunton, Va., June 14, 2007.

Farrell II, Thomas F. "Energy Debates, Past, Present, and Future: This Time Can We Be Honest With Ourselves?" Photocopied speech. Regent University Executive Leadership Series. Virginia Beach, Va., Mar. 20, 2007.

Farrell II, Thomas F. "Remarks." Photocopied speech. Clean Energy Task Force, National Governors Association. Washington, D.C., Feb. 23, 2008.

Farrell II, Thomas F. "Climate Change: EEI Wall Street Briefing." Photocopied speech. June 13, 2007.

The Gift of Caring. Brochure. 2007.

"History of Labor Relations: 1935–1966." Virginia Electric and Power Company.

"Important Dates in History." Photocopy of undated internal document.

The Never Ending Story… Virginia Electric and Power Company. Undated.

PoweringVirginia. www.poweringvirginia.com

Powerline (1986–88). Dominion Resources, Inc.

Public Service News (1916–1927). Virginia Railway and Power Company.

Smith, Nancy L. and P. Lee Starkey. *The VNG Story*. Virginia Natural Gas. Undated.

The Vepcovian (1927–1964). Virginia Electric and Power Company.

Virginia Electric and Power Company Annual Reports (1925–1984).

Virginia Natural Gas. www.virginianaturalgas.com/Universal/AboutUs.aspx.

WRVA AM. Wartime Radio PSA. Richmond, circa early 1940s.

OTHER SOURCES

Freeman, Anne Hobson. "T. Justin Moore." *Style of a Law Firm: Eight Gentlemen From Virginia*. Chapel Hill, N.C.: Algonquin Books of Chapel Hill, 1989. 132–37.

Henderson, William D. "Rapids and Power: The Appomattox River and Electrical Power in Petersburg, Virginia." *Virginia Cavalcade* (Spring 1978): 153.

Hudson, Richard L. "Generating Grief." *The Wall Street Journal* (Oct. 23, 1979): 1.

Sanford, Jack K. "Richmond: Her Triumphs, Tragedies & Growth." Richmond: Metropolitan Richmond Chamber of Commerce. Undated.

"Staff Investigation of the Restructuring of the Electric Industry." Virginia State Corporation Commission. www.scc.virginia.gov/news/restrct3.htm (Sept. 2007).

"The Story of Rural Electrification." *The Ground Beneath Our Feet: Virginia's History Since the Civil War*. May 14, 2009. www.vahistory.org/electrification.html.

"Virginia Electric and Power Company: History of Collective Bargaining." IBEW files. Undated.

Will, Erwin H. "The Past — Interesting, The Present — Intriguing, The Future — Bright: A Story of Virginia Electric and Power Company." Published speech. Virginia Dinner of the Newcomen Society in North America, Richmond, Va., Apr. 1965. ■

AUTHOR'S ACKNOWLEDGMENTS

Many Dominion team members pitched in to make this book possible. Thank you all: Patty Wilkerson and Irene Cimino, my knowledgeable primary contacts who helped clarify the book's themes during the planning stage and provided research support and encouragement right up to press time; Katie Murray for her willingness to track down the most esoteric facts; Becky Worley, Jessica Price, and Phil Graham for their research assistance; Martha J. Uzel and Anne M. Justis for arranging travel; everyone who lent memorabilia and artifacts (listed in the Image Credits); and the Dominion editorial and image selection teams, some of whom were interviewed — Carl Baab, Jim Evans, Mark Lazenby, Jim Norvelle, Landon Simpson, Lora Spiller, Chet Wade, and John Wiley.

Also invaluable were the recollections of many retirees, interviewed by Jim Babb and the West Cary Group as they produced a Dominion centennial exhibit with a photo scrapbook, audio files, and videos. Additional quotes and images from these simultaneously produced projects have enhanced this book. And I extend appreciation to the Virginia Historical Society and the Library of Virginia for their expert help.

Special thanks to all interviewees:

Harold Adams
John Ahladas
Danny Allen
David Allen
Herman Allen
Monte Allen
Lola Ausby
Cindy Balderson
Mike Barclay
William Bartlow
Bill Berry
Virginia Board
Frank Brayton
William Brooks
Dixie Bryant
Bob Burrus
Tom Capps
Demetrius Carter
Tom Chewning
Bill Crump
George Davidson

Lovic Davis
Mike Duffey
Buddy Earley
Pam Faggert
Rosemary Fahed
Tom Farrell II
Susan Gardner
Marjorie Grier
Tom Hamlin
Eva Teig Hardy
Paul Hilton
Craig Ivey
Tom Jarvis
Jay Johnson
Allan Jones
Benny Lambert
J. B. Lankes
Cliff Newman
Randy McIver
Lyn McDermid
Becky Merritt
Bill Mistr
Jay Moore
Ev Munsey

George O'Connell
Bucky Oates
Marlin Patrick
Jim Rhodes
Linwood Robertson
Charlie Rudasill
Randy Sizemore
Pam Snider
Lee Starkey
K. B. Tillman
Jack Wells
Milton Woodlief
Nancy Woodlief
Keith Wooldridge
Floyd Yates

Appreciation is also extended to others who contributed their time and expertise to the project:

Viki Armentrout
Max Bartholomew
Pete Beament
Rodney Blevins
Anna Brooks
Sharon Burr
Ed Bushee
Bill Byrd
Steve Chafin
Joyce Collins
John Croslin
Anita Cullop-Thompson
Frances Daniel
Kevin Dobbins
Charlie Donato
Dan Donovan
Lenny Dupuis
Charles Ellison
Oswald Gasser
Walter George
Bill Hall

Rebecca Heller
Kent Hill
J. J. Hoard
Rosalyn Hobson
Kathleen Holmes
Kellie Holmes
Bonnie Horton
Ray Hugo
Michael Isper
Jack Kerr
Mark Kilduff
Fred King
David Koogler
Leslie Krieg
Justine Lloyd
Brenda Long
Kim Lowers
Cal Lucy
Dennis McDade
Gary Miller
Lisa Moerner
Kim Mueller
Rebecca Neal
Bob Newman
Jason Newman
Nikki Nicholau
Carla Picard

Henry Poindexter
Jim Poland
Anita Powell
Kristen Reese
F. Scott Reed
Lee Reed
Carter Reid
Bob Rigsby
David Robinson
Steve Rogers
Sarah Scott
Joann Shriner
John Smatlak
Chester Smith
Ray Sommerfeld
Vincent Sutphin
Bill Thompson
John Thurston
Melissa Totten
James Wellons
Ann Wilder
Bob Williams
Tom Wohlfarth
Carol Zedaker

ABOUT THE AUTHOR

Heidi Tyline King earned a journalism degree from the University of Alabama. She has written books and magazine articles on a variety of nonfiction topics ranging from holiday celebrations to biographies to travel. Her company history work includes books for several corporations and nonprofit organizations, including another CorporateHistory.net compilation celebrating the 75th anniversary of Advance Auto Parts in Roanoke, Virginia. Heidi lives in Florida with her husband, geologist Creed King, and their daughters.

IMAGE CREDITS

Copyright and Contents spread: Dementi Studio

7: Doug Buerlein (photo of Tom Farrell)

9: Dementi Studio

11: Library of Congress, George Grantham Bain Collection (top); courtesy of Carter Peaseley (bottom)

13: Courtesy of Lovic Davis (artifacts and photo)

14: Dementi Studio

16: Tidewater Photo Service, Inc.

17: Dementi Studio (men's team)

18: Courtesy of Scott Kinzie (postcards)

20: Dementi Studio

21: Dementi Studio

22: Courtesy of Susan Gardner (top); Boice Studios (center); Edison Electric Institute (bottom)

23: Gladstone Studio (top)

24: The Reddy Kilowatt Corporation (center)

25: Courtesy of Frances Daniel (bill and envelope)

26: Courtesy of Frances Daniel (plaque); Dementi Studio (top)

28: Dementi Studio / Photo by A. L. Dementi (top); courtesy of Rosemary Fahed (pins)

29: U.S. Coast Guard Public Relations Office, Fifth Naval District

30: Courtesy of Fred King (center)

31: *Richmond Times-Dispatch* (cartoon by Gary Brookins); Cameron Davidson (bottom)

33: Courtesy of Thomas M. Balacke (center); Library of Virginia (top right, bottom right)

34: Courtesy of Lee Starkey (lapel pin); Tim Wright (top right)

35: Courtesy of Lee Starkey (photos) — Long's Photo Service (top center); Tim Wright (bottom)

36: Courtesy of Becky Worley (magazine cover); Le Roy Anderson (photo)

37: David Allen

38: Courtesy of *The EL&P Gazette* (newspaper)

39: *Richmond Times-Dispatch* (top right)

41: Doug Buerlein (center right); John Henley (bottom)

42: Mark Mitchell (bottom)

43: Bob Jones Jr. (bottom)

44: Old Dominion University, Henry Howell Collection (newspaper); © Cameron Davidson / Corbis (top right)

47: Courtesy of Bob Rigsby (tie and belt buckle)

51: *Richmond Times-Dispatch* (clippings)

53: © Living Earth/Spaceshots

55: Library of Congress (far left)

57: Ben Spiegel (bottom)

58: Chip Mitchell

61: Courtesy of Dixie Bryant (top); courtesy of Bob Newman (bottom)

65: Joe Glick (top left)

67: Mark Mitchell (bottom)

68: Courtesy of Jack Wells (artifacts)

69: Joe Glick

71: Richmond Newspapers, Inc. (top left); courtesy of Allen Black (top right)

73: Doug Beurlein (top right)

74: The Reddy Kilowatt Corporation; courtesy of Rosemary Fahed (tie clasp, nightlight, figurine)

75: The Reddy Kilowatt Corporation; courtesy of Rosemary Fahed (card); courtesy of Bill Crump (photo bottom right and cartoon top right by Jeff MacNelly)

79: Courtesy of Eva Hardy

82: Dementi Studio (bottom)

84: Doug Buerlein (top)

85: Dementi Studio (top right)

88: Doug Buerlein (bottom left); Bob Jones Jr. (top right)

89: Courtesy of University of Virginia Press (book cover)

90: Zaidan Photography (top left)

92: Mark Mitchell

94: Michael Goodman

95: Cameron Davidson

98: Courtesy of *Corporate Responsibility Officer* magazine (top left)

99: Cameron Davidson (top); William Taufic (bottom)

103: Cameron Davidson

104: Cameron Davidson

105: David Allen (top); Cameron Davidson (inset)

106: Doug Buerlein (top)

109: Cameron Davidson

110: PJM Interconnection (map)

111: Lee Brauer

112: David Allen (center); Doug Buerlein (bottom)

113: Photo Craftsmen, Inc. (center)

114: David Allen (top); C. H. Ruth, courtesy of Scott Kinzie (bottom)

116: Cameron Davidson (top); Bill Ruffner (bottom)

All other images and artifacts appear courtesy of Dominion.

Photography of artifacts by Mark Mitchell

Adobe® Photoshop® services by David Ridderhof

INDEX

Page numbers appear in boldface for illustrations.

VEPCO's diamond logo had its roots in a 1924 emblem
designed by Virginia Railway and Power Company
engineer William W. Jones. The railway company became
VEPCO in 1925, and the logo evolved with minor changes
until it was replaced by an all-type version in the 1960s
and the Virginia Power logo in 1985. Dominion's current
logo made its debut in 2000.